# Light, Fire, & ABUNDANCE

# *Light, Fire, &* ABUNDANCE

HARNESS THE POWER OF FOOD & MINDFUL COOKING TO NOURISH THE BODY & SOUL

## MISTY BELL STIERS

FOREWORD BY DAWN AURORA HUNT

PHOTOGRAPHY BY JUAN PATIÑO

APOLLO
PUBLISHERS

*For Samaire and Wylie, may the recipes in these pages always bring you home when you most need it, no matter where or when.*

# Contents

# Foreword

## by Dawn Aurora Hunt

*Kitchen Witch, Author, and Owner of Cucina Aurora Kitchen Witchery*

**WHAT COMES TO MIND** when you think about cooking or food? When I think about cooking, I am transported into my kitchen, where my feet are firmly planted on the floor as soft jazz wafts through the air scented with the aroma of the garlic and onions sautéing in my sacred space. When I think about food, I am transported into my grandmother's kitchen in the height of summer. Bright yellow vinyl chairs stick to my nine-year-old self in the humidity, while my grandmother tears fresh basil leaves to toss with peppers roasting over the open flame of the gas stove. Cooking is inspiration, possibilities, and creativity—endless combinations of flavor, texture, and technique that excite the senses and create foods to fill the belly. The process of creating meals and sharing food with others is so important and one I revere. When I think about food and cooking, I realize they are my magic.

Throughout the COVID-19 pandemic lockdowns, there was a marked uptick in people rediscovering the art and magic of cooking. There was a renewed fascination with things like bread baking, home brewing, and meals shared together. When the lockdowns ended, we rushed back to restaurants and the homes of others to share meals and make memories with those we love. Lately there is so much divisiveness and anger in the world. I sometimes think that if I could just make a big enough lasagna, we could all sit down together and realize that there is so much more that we have in common than that makes us different. We all must eat to survive, regardless of our spiritual path, sexual orientation, gender identity, or race. This is one of the most basic, most beautiful reminders of our sameness, of our bond as human beings.

As a practicing kitchen witch for the better part of two decades, I've taught classes and seen many people light up when the discussions turn to food, nurturing, and cooking. Misty is one such person. A chance meeting in New York City over a decade ago led to a long-distance, long-standing friendship full of mutual respect and a deep love of good food. When I heard she was writing a magical cookbook, I was very excited to see what enchanting entrées she'd cook up. After years of cooking, teaching, and writing on kitchen witchery, even I need to get inspired from time to time.

Seeing kitchen and food magic through the meals of Misty, I am transported from my own kitchen to places held in my heart I had forgotten. It is with a renewed sense of wonder and human connection that I read Misty's writing, and I now long to cook big meals surrounded by smiling faces. Just as delicious food can be a transcendent experience, so too is the art of making it with mindfulness and magic. Cooking your way through this book is like getting an in-depth journey into the soul of another person, the soul of a kitchen witch whose love of family, nurturing, memory, and tradition can be felt (and tasted) in each bite. Misty's recipes and witchcraft intermingle with flavorful prose to inspire your own magical, alchemical, and culinary dreams, with accessible instructions for the beginner or the well-seasoned kitchen witch. Diving into these pages, you will find deep connection with food, magic, and your own practices of nurturing home and family. Like a meal shared with friends, you'll finish this book with a fulfilled heart and satisfied soul.

# Introduction

**I REMEMBER THE MOMENT** I received what would eventually become my grimoire, my family record, one of my most treasured possessions. Sam, my husband, had wrapped it how he wraps all gifts, using a brown paper bag, folded over at the edges, with no tape or ribbon to speak of. Thoughtfully chosen, distractedly encased.

I pulled the gift from the bag and then caught my breath as I soaked it in. It was a small, worn leather recipe book carefully held closed with a braided leather ribbon. The front was engraved with the words "3rd Anniversary Misty & Sam October 29, 2005," and my fingers trailed over them, feeling their slight raise on the soft leather of the cover. As I opened the book, I found that inside was a collection of small plastic sleeves and an assortment of matching blank notecards. The book was brand-new, yet soft and worn—like it had been passed between generations—and welcoming, with the comfort of home. It would be a place to record our history. This gift was recognition of our past and a promise of so many tomorrows. I held it close to my heart and wondered at all we would fill it with.

Today, well over a decade later, the book is filled with memories, notes, and a couple of letters to Santa. It has magazine clippings and small photos, all bunched in with lists of dates and memories. Oh, and recipes. So many recipes. Hastily written. Carefully scribed. All manner of meals and celebrations.

It's so much more than a card catalog of meals. In many ways it's our life together, a collection of Saturday mornings and Tuesday evenings, birthdays, holidays, and everydays saved and curated, loved and remembered, referenced and held close. The big ones, the small ones. A diary of our lives, how we felt, who we shared our time with. And a few dreams for tomorrow.

I can turn the small plastic sleeves and relive my son Wylie's first meal, the card smudged and spotted. I can run my fingers over the ingredients of the first dinner Sam and I ever made together. When time moves too fast, I can sit with the letters of a child's studious and sprawling handwriting titling my daughter Samaire's first recipe.

Most of the cards are filled with my own supine script, but there are a few notable exceptions aside from Samaire's childhood alphabet, like Sam's mom's rhubarb pie recipe recorded on her husband's work stationary, and my mother's recording of my grandmother's recipe for chocolate pudding cake. The narrative of this tome stretches across time and place, across generations.

If I can be called a witch with a spell book, it would be in reference to my reliance on this book. It is the book I consult when I am in need of something intangible. A moment of comfort or remembrance. A time relived. A celebration of something new. This book can transport me instantly to a past moment and is a quiet place to dream of what's to come.

It's all there in that book with the worn leather binding. And now some of it is here, in this book too. I hope that within these pages you will find comfort, that you will find ways to create joy, solace, reverie, and peace. Maybe this book will inspire you to take a moment and a deep calming breath in the midst of an everyday chore. Maybe it will allow you to feel more present and connected to those who are dear to you, and, most importantly, to yourself. I hope so.

I hope, too, that you fill this book with notes, scribbles, and memories. And that maybe, just maybe, you begin your own small collection of moments to remember and hold close that just happen to be meals.

## FINDING THE MAGIC THAT RESTS AT YOUR TABLE

Finding your magic in the kitchen, like anywhere else, is about being present. It's about being in the moment enough to make intentional choices about what your heart and soul need, or what you want to provide for those around you. It's about love—loving yourself and those whom you choose to make your world—by creating something with your hands that comes from your heart.

Food provides comfort and nourishes us; not just our bodies, but our beings. The smells from certain meals can transport us across miles to those we love, transport us to another time, break the barriers between this world and the next, bringing us close to those we have lost. Certain tastes can ignite our senses, warming us from the inside out, bringing light and fire and abundance. We can find comfort, too, in the perfect cup of tea or slice of warm bread—even in the time we take to knead the dough or steep the leaves.

Cooking is a special kind of alchemy. A way to take disparate ingredients and through an act of intention combine them to create something that wasn't there before. Something new and uniquely ours. Not just something to consume, but something to experience. Not just a meal, but an act of love filled with your own special kind of magic.

You don't need to be a witch to impart that magic. In fact, most people already have their own traditions, rituals, or magical kitchen practices.

The salt thrown over the shoulder.

The "bit of spice" for luck.

The recipe for when someone has a cold, or something to celebrate.

The special dessert that gets made every holiday.

Sometimes it's the ingredients that are significant, sometimes it's when a dish is made that matters. Always the magic is in the how and who. A beloved ingredient, a special bowl or plate, a mother's touch, an uncle's spices, a friend's thoughtfulness. These meals and recipes grow special because they began with an intention, a presence of mind, and a generosity of spirit that follows them over time. And so that is where the magic of the kitchen resides: in the ability to be intentional in what you're making, consciously choosing the result of your endeavor. Comfort? Hope? Encouragement? Love? Intent is realized in a million different ways, in every decision you make as you prepare your food.

Is every meal an exercise in the divine? Every mac and cheese a call to a greater power? Hardly. I spend a great deal of time desperately trying to get a meal in front of my kids that has some semblance of nutrition, that everyone will eat at least some of, and that can be completely prepared and served in that wisp of time between the end of my workday and the beginning of their bedtime.

To say I'm always intentional would be a gross overstatement. But there are small rituals that can helps us slow our rush of days and recognize this act of making a meal for what it is: a unique daily opportunity to be present. It is a time to give to ourselves and those we care for. If only for a moment, it is a way to let go of what we did earlier in the day, release the pressure of what may come, and just live in the now. It is a way to feed our bodies and acknowledge our souls in the midst of something we have to do anyway.

Whether opening a can of chicken and stars or lovingly crafting a homemade masterpiece, we have the opportunity to take a moment to appreciate where we are and what it means that we have this food in front of us, this opportunity to nourish. We have an opportunity to take a breath and give thanks, share love, and choose how the meal could evolve into a moment. Even if it is just a moment piled on the couch watching a cartoon and slurping star-shaped noodles in spaghetti-like sauce out of a can.

## KITCHEN RITUAL

Kitchen witches find their greatest peace and comfort in the rituals of preparing food and channeling their intentions in the kitchen. Often kitchen witches are also healers, drawing upon the natural properties of plants and herbs to help ameliorate physical and psychological ailments. But recognizing that the meaning and rituals that live in all our kitchens are sacred isn't the honor of the kitchen witch alone. When any of us makes a meal for someone we love, creating a dish to comfort or encourage, we are enjoying a sacred act. Creating something with our hands to nourish the heart and soul is a gift, a treasure filled with the utmost magic, no matter what spiritual path we may follow.

Meals are opportunities for everyone to create with intent, to infuse meaning into a dish, into a gathering. Everyone is capable of choosing ingredients with intention, carefully planning meals, and embracing sigils (symbols that invoke certain kinds of power, such as the ones we have carried with us since childhood breakfast—hearts and clover, stars and moons) to be stirred into soups, traced out with a spoon in pancake batter, carved into the top of a loaf of bread. By doing so, we recognize and acknowledge the wonder in this world, and then we harness that wonder and create some enchantment ourselves. This means being in tune with the energy around us but also trusting the energy in our hearts, listening to our intuition, the whispering of our souls, and finding a way to share a piece of ourselves with the outside world.

This kind of magic is nothing otherworldly. Often it simply means doing what needs to be done. In this way, we are able to relieve a bit of the pain of someone who is hurting, carry a bit of their burden when we have the strength to spare—and sometimes even when we don't. It also means noticing someone who feels lost, and truly making them feel seen; holding the hand of one who might need to borrow some courage; or baking bread for someone who needs to feel loved. This kind of witchery isn't conjuring, it's connecting. It's not about having a third eye or second sight; rather, it's about taking the time to see what is truly around you and choosing to make it better, lovelier, and kinder by offering up a gift only you can give. It is a token woven with time, effort, and intention. It is not just invoking, it is involving. It is deciding to be a force in the world we inhabit, to be an active part of the wondrous cycle that moves us all. It is making the choice to create in the hope of balancing, banishing, or brightening.

Finding your magic is so much more than performing spells and practicing concoctions to bring money, love, or luck. It's about *being* the wealth and love needed, for yourself as well as those around you, and making your own luck by seizing opportunities and recognizing moments of synchronicity. This is so much more than the dull, expected definition of what is magical. It is empowering yourself to join in a greater force to become truly mystical and learn that even the smallest of offerings can create the most memorable and life-changing moments whose effects will linger long after the dishes are cleared.

## INGREDIENTS AND INTENTIONS

Part of cooking with intention and bringing magic to all your dishes is your selection of ingredients. What will bring comfort? How can you infuse love or incite bravery? What will bring calm and help a tired heart? If you do enough research you find that certain ingredients have been recorded as being consistently used to achieve specific outcomes. Others, not so much. And still more yield so very many uses that you start to feel like following that particular rabbit hole may be endless.

Since the first meal was made, humans have imbued meaning and imparted feeling into the composition—whether trying to give strength to survive the day or simply bring a good night's sleep. We all do it still, if a bit unconsciously at times, reaching for old favorites or beloved recipes—the chicken soup for sickness, the cake for celebration, the cookies for a magical midnight snack over the holidays. We throw a thimble of turmeric into the pot because that's what Grandma always did. We add the pinch of cinnamon and sugar over the berries because our kids love "fairy berries" and it makes us (and them) smile. We move bowls with a lifetime of memories attached across our counters. We embrace flavors that bring up moments we cherish and people we miss.

Of course, we all also have meals and moments we'd rather forget. Do we not all have that one meal we would like to leave languishing in the tomes of history? The recipe gone wrong, the meal that forever turned us against its unsuspecting courses. Or those moments when our adventure, or rather misadventure, perhaps fell a bit short? The cake surprisingly filled with chunks of beets, or the Ooey Gooey Butter Cake (see page 237) with a truly gooey end to it.

We all have missteps along our culinary journeys. I could fill this book with mine, though I'll spare us both the trouble. Our mistakes and misadventures are as much a part of our magic and making as our glorious triumphs. In the end, though, it's the magic that endures, that shapes us. Not because of a list of ingredients but because of the moments they lead to.

I offer up the list below as a starting point, a place to seek inspiration when you know how you wish to feel or what you wish to impart but not necessarily what you want to eat. Explore the meanings of your favorite ingredients and add your own notes for what they mean to you. Making a meal is a truly incredible chance to take time you spend doing an everyday task and transform it into an instant you can slow down for, be present in, and be conscious of. All you need is a small sprinkle for luck, a dash for love, a spoonful of magic.

## GENERAL GUIDELINES

Greens (lettuce, spinach, kale, collards) are often associated with money. It feels right, does it not? Not only does the color correspond here in North America, but these all grow in bunches, leading to a feeling of abundance, an inference of wealth. Rarely, if ever, do we use this particular ingredient singularly. Rather, we grab glorious clusters to add to our meals.

Peppers and spice are linked closely with passion and love. Peppers come in all forms and intensities, but they all raise our temperature just a bit. Some peppers give off a quick shot of heat, not long but intense. Others linger, warming us on the inside in a way that seems to permeate our very being. Lust and love. Passion and pleasure. The hot touch of that initial and sometimes lasting connection made tangible in just a simple savor.

Pungent herbs and spices (think garlic and onions) are often linked to protection. This always brings me joy, because the child in me will never not associate garlic with vampires. But it makes sense: these ingredients are often ones we temper as to not drive away those closest. Their aromas not only stick to our fingers, our clothes, and even our hair, but infiltrate our very breath. Eat too much and you'll have plenty of space to yourself! A natural force field. And while the folkloric protection offered is symbolic more than a result of questionable breath, it's easy to see where this particular symbology came from.

## SPECIFICS

### ALLSPICE
Energy and determination, revitalization

### ALMOND
Heightened sense of purpose, wisdom

### APPLE
Immortality, longevity

### ARTICHOKE
Patience, a reminder that our journey should be joyful

### BANANA
Resilience through change, adaptability

### BASIL
Prosperity, love, divination

**BAY LEAF**

Strength, healing, manifestation of abundance

**BELL PEPPER (GREEN OR RED)**

Desire and love, a subtle sweetness

**BLACK BEAN**

Clarity and truth, assists in making important decisions

**BLACKBERRY**

Prosperity, tenacity

**BLACK PEPPER**

Courage, banishes negativity

**BLUEBERRY**

Peace, calm, acceptance

**BROCCOLI AND BROCCOLINI**

Growth, love and trust in oneself, enables the path to solutions for seemingly immutable problems

**CARROT**

Creativity, eliminates fear of being authentic

**CAULIFLOWER**

Reminder of our multitudes, associated with the moon and feminine energy

**CAYENNE**

Sustained well-being, motivation, a remover of obstacles

**CHEESE**

Transforms, deepens complexity, knowledge

**CHERRY**

Acts as a reminder of the fleeting space of time, symbolizes our own short but glorious existence, evanescence

**CHOCOLATE**

Love in all its forms; white chocolate imbues self-love, milk chocolate solidifies friendship and nurtures, dark chocolate ignites passion, and romance

**CINNAMON**

Enhances love, amplifies intuition, incites exploration

**CLEMENTINE**

Joy, creativity

**CLOVE**

Attracts friendship, clears negativity, protects dreams

**CORIANDER AND CILANTRO**

Promote peace, healing, love

**CORN**

Divination, insight

**CRANBERRY**

Opens communication

**CUCUMBER**

Healing, youthfulness

**CUMIN**

Guards against thievery,

offers protection

**DATE**

Symbol of the soul, resurrection

**DILL**

Soothes, calms, protects from

bad dreams

**ELDERBERRY**

Connects us to our ancestors,

releases enchantments,

provides clear sight

**GARLIC**

Protection

**GINGER**

Draws out adventure and new

experiences, promotes

sensuality, sexuality,

personal confidence

**GRAPEFRUIT**

Releases confusion,

aids clarity,

clears space for

self-love

**GREEN ONION/SCALLION**

Adaptability, protection

**HONEY**

Sweetly binding, stability,

longevity, sweetness, passion

**HOPS**

Heals, provides rest, acts as

a door between worlds

**KALE**

Longevity, prosperity

**LEEK**

Protects and strengthens

existing love

**LEMON**

Deters misfortune, provides

refreshment and rejuvenation

**LENTIL**

Financial security

**LIME**

Purification, luck

**MAPLE**

Provides balance, enables

generosity

**MARJORAM**

Protection from discord

**MILK**

Symbol of motherhood,

fertility, abundance

**MINT**

Encourages wakefulness

and concentration,

protects travelers

**MUSTARD**

Reminder that greatness can

come from small things,

disrupts trouble

**NAVY BEAN**

Security

**NORTHERN (WHITE) BEAN**

Brings discovery and insight,
protects plans

**NUTMEG**

Clairvoyance, insight

**ONION**

Represents the infinite universe,
sacred to the moon, uncovers
and unmasks problems and
possibilities

**ORANGE**

Joy, prosperity, success

**OREGANO**

Mountains of joy, happiness,
success

**PAPRIKA**

Boosts intentions and spell work

**PARSLEY**

Eases grief, honors the dead

**PEANUT**

Unification, power, immortality

**PEAR**

Elicits love

**PECAN**

Success, job security

**PEPPER (CAPSICUM)**

Poblano, Habanero, Serrano,
Chipotle, Jalapeño, Red Pepper
Flakes

Provides passion and energy,
increases courage, deters evil

**PEPPERMINT**

Healing, purification, protection

**PINE NUT**

Promotes clean breaks, resilience,
supports new beginnings, success

**PINTO BEAN**

Promotes action and forward
movement

**POPPY SEED**

Tenacity, heightened awareness

**POTATO**

Provides grounding,
protection, stability

**PUMPKIN, PUMPKIN SEED,
SQUASH**

Enables summoning, provides
prosperity, wards against
malevolence

**RADISH**

Protects against curses,
imbues balance of energy

**RASPBERRY**

Fertility, love

**RED BEAN**

Wisdom, healing

**ROSEMARY**

Aids remembrance,
increases fidelity
and memory

**SAFFRON**

Protects, guards, wards off evil

**SAGE**

Purifies, cleanses, wards off evil, most powerful when gifted

**SESAME**

Money, lust, passion

**SHALLOT**

Cures misfortune, brings luck

**SPINACH**

Strength, endurance, helps to lay the groundwork to take action

**STRAWBERRY**

Special magic, favorite food of the fair folk, sign of love, dedication; triple leaves are a sign of the goddess

**SUGAR**

Dispels evil, enhances love, lust

**SWEET POTATO**

Provides grounding, friendship, harmony

**TARRAGON**

Aids in gaining influence, power, and control

**THYME**

Bravery, courage, clarity

**TOMATILLO**

Steadies the heart

**TOMATO**

Opens the heart, reveals opportunities for love and friendship, encourages generosity, and the giving and receiving of love

**TURMERIC**

Energy, vitality

**VANILLA**

Soothes, calms, aids in personal empowerment

**VINEGAR**

Fire energy, protection

**WALNUT**

Removes obstructions, expellant, exoneration

**ZUCCHINI**

Tenacity, assertiveness, aids in difficult tasks

## COOKING WHEN IT COUNTS

In the rush of the everyday, it is easy to feel disconnected, to let hours, days, and even weeks slip by unnoticed or at least unrecognized and uncelebrated. It is easy to fall into the habit of hours, marching through errands, chores, and obligations with such alacrity that an interruption from the norm has us stop to look around, shocked we don't know what day it is exactly or that the week has flown by unexpectedly.

In the rush of the everyday, it can feel increasingly hard to be present, difficult to root ourselves in the moment we are in, because we are so busy replaying the moments before or planning for the moments on the way. And yet it is when we are aware, in the now, that we can feel our own magic, appreciate the wonder around us, operate with purpose in even the smallest acts of our lives, and gift ourselves the ability to be present. This is the gift of being able to revel in the sounds of birds outside the window or the lay of light on the counter, of taking the time to truly listen to the person in front of us or just giving ourselves a moment to be, to breathe, to find what we need—joy, respite, or relaxation.

I find I am at my best when I can let go of what has gone before, release a little of what's to come, and sit in the moment I am in. It helps me feel closer to those I love and gives me time to take care of myself. But this is not a random action, an unexpected occurrence; it's a choice I have to make, and admittedly it's not one I make enough.

When I feel my days start to grow a bit out of control, when the hours slip by and the weeks tumble over one another, I also feel less connected to myself, to my loved ones, to the greater world around me. I start to feel a bit lost, unmoored. These moments find me reaching for my tattered leather grimoire, the scraps of paper, the bits of meals. I am searching for something specific, something to remind me that I am part of the world as it turns, traveling through the seasons on the wheel of the year and experiencing the movement of the sun across the sky, living alongside the narrative of life and light, darkness and resolution, hope and rebirth. The meals I make tie me to those larger things and connect me, resolutely, to where I need to be.

The reminder that time was passing by used to be clear from what we found on our shelves, what we placed on our plates. But I now live, with great fortune, in a place where the food of the seasons is readily available year-round. There are very few items I can't track down at any time of year if I really want them. Still, there's something special about eating a food when it's meant to be eaten, when its harvest naturally occurs. There is a ritual of sorts that happens in the finding, getting, and preparing of foods that appear when the sun is at its highest, or when the leaves crunch beneath our shoes. The act is a reminder that time is fleeting, the world is turning, and we deserve to be a part of it all.

I look forward every year to the asparagus risotto (see page 113) that tastes especially wonderful in the spring when the crocuses are just poking out from the frost and snow, to the warmth of the pumpkin muffins (see page 219) and pies that fill our home with delicious aromas when the days turn brief, and to the strawberries covered in cream (see page 223) that fill our bowls in the summer, a sweet respite from the heat that rises into our fifth-floor walk-up. Most of all, I love the dreaming it allows. Every fall we drive a few hours north to tromp through Pennings Orchard searching for the perfect apples. We spend a glorious afternoon running, wandering, and exploring up and down the great aisles, seeking out the perfect ripe apples. The kids stop and read every sign posted at the end of the rows describing each type of apple to be found. Gala, Red Delicious, Empire, Golden . . . tart to sweet, sour, and honeyed. Great plans are made between the trees as they scramble beneath branches weighted heavily, future pies concocted as Sam stands on his toes and raises his arm, reaching higher and higher for the perfect shining apple on the tallest branch. Each apple carefully selected into service.

The apples are then thrown together into giant netted bags, all the individual taste profiles perfectly forgotten as we gather our bounty. It happens every year. Every year we discuss an alternate system. Photos to record what is what? Separate, labeled bags? But half the fun, we all know, is returning home to pull out each apple and guess what kind it is as we plan how we will fill the weeks ahead with empanadas, pies, cobblers, and sauces. Those apples, those meals, are a gateway to the fall. A sign to change what's in our closets, bring out our coats, make sure everyone has boots that fit. They are a marker in time and a way to stop and luxuriate in the cooling of our evenings, the early arrival of the stars, the coming eruption of color in our trees.

Seasonal cooking can do that. It reminds us of where we are, connecting us to the changing of the seasons and the stories being told. Finding the perfect strawberries and sitting beneath the sun, juice dripping down, exhausted from a day of exploration and laughter, is a token of the brightest of days, a celebration of the bounty of the light, time, and warmth we have. In colder weather, we delight in the warmth of cinnamon and nutmeg, in cozy fires, in the deep nights of the winter filled with slow stews and quiet evenings. These are small suggestions that the world is slowing, resting, coalescing, and comforting for a time, a permission to be at ease.

We need not wait, however, for the seasons to turn for guidance on what and how food can connect us to our world and the people in it. The very turn of our days and nights can offer that up as well. Every night we get the perfect advice on what direction to take our current repast. The moon offers a rhythm and reason in her journey through the stars. Over and over she reminds us of the need and benefit of conscious change, of perpetual movement, and of the need to honor ourselves in whatever state we may be in. She gives us reason to pause and reflect on intent.

And in all honesty, when I'm at the end of my rope and can't for the life of me figure out what to make for dinner, I often open up my moon app on my phone and check what stage we're in. (I know! I should just *know*, right? I should be able to tell you at any point if we're waxing, waning, or full. I'm such a waste of a witch for a friend some times. But I can always quickly find the info on my phone, and so can you.)

The moon is a great resource to help you stay connected to your hopes and aspirations. She is a tool to guide you in building the life you want. As she waxes in the sky, growing bigger every moment, think about what you'd like more of in your life. Go ahead and add those vegetables you have been avoiding. Finally try that new fish recipe. Welcome in new habits and ways of thinking. Bake some homemade bread. Make a Dutch baby pancake (see page 34). Remind yourself of the beauty and joy of rising to the occasion. Fulfill promises you have made to yourself and make meals that reflect who you are, who you love, who you want to be. Make foods that fill you with promise and hope: embrace clementines for joy and creativity, raspberries and strawberries for love.

As the moon wanes, we are offered the chance to reflect on what we'd like to let go of. Behaviors that don't suit us. Practices that no longer bring us joy. Let them go. Stop stressing over fixing the perfect meal and revel in just getting something on the table. Release a few worries, put distance between you and that which doesn't serve your goals and aspirations. Commit to the evolution of understanding that letting go doesn't mean leaving behind but prioritizing what we need over what we feel obligated to do. Make some pesto with walnuts to help remove obstacles and spinach for endurance (see page 276), or use pine nuts (see page 278) for a good old-fashioned clean break. Find food that will make you feel strong and resilient. Food nourishes our bodies, but it acts as a physical reminder of behavior and intent too. Leverage that and choose ingredients to serve you. Intentionally feed your soul.

The dark or new moon makes space to go inward to explore your heart and your soul. In a world of constant demands, taking a moment to follow the moon's example to go dark for a bit is imperative. Allow yourself to rest, to retreat and renew. Make yourself a soup, stew, or sauce that you can set on the stove and let culminate without you. Put some berries, cream, and cake together and let the treat set in a cool place to become delicious. Release and rest. Find food that entices you to look inward, to let the world go spinning madly on as you seek out your purpose and path without obligation or expectation.

And, of course, there's the point at which the moon's light fills the sky—bright, undaunted, and courageous. You too have light to share. Celebrate that. Live the reminder the moon provides. Find ingredients that make you feel your best, your brightest. Fill your plate with golden food. Make beautifully round pizzas and pies and fill and top them with abundance. Remind yourself of all that you have and all that you are as a gift to this world, and celebrate.

I once read a social media post that stated that the worst part of being an adult is figuring out what dinner will be every night. I feel that in my bones. But making the conscious choice of how I want to spend the time to make it, how I want that meal to serve me—not just to fill my stomach but to fill my heart—makes this chore just a bit easier.

There will always be days I give up and order delivery. Days when I pull a pizza out of the freezer or slap a loaf of bread and peanut butter on the counter next to a bag of carrots and tell my kids they are on their own. But when I can, I try to take a moment to seek out what I need, how I can ground myself and choose to be connected, and follow the paths and seasons of the world around me. Even if it is just grabbing the strawberry jam to place next to the peanut butter as a small token of love.

Sunny-Side Up

*Sunny-Side Up*

# BREAKFAST

**I THINK OF BREAKFAST** less as a meal reflecting a time of day and more as a way to relish a new beginning. There is a special place a traditional breakfast meal can transport you to—memories of lazy mornings and bright cartoons, feelings of creeping sunshine and endless possibility. It can bring back that moment before you are fully awake, drifting into the delicious aroma of someone else's act of love simmering just beyond the door—simply awaiting your arrival to the day.

I love these meals and the feeling they impart. The hope and brightness they can lend, whether the day has yet to break or the night has already fallen. I hope these recipes bring some of that light to you. The feeling that anything is possible and the reminder that another chance, another day, another sunrise is just around the corner.

# Fluffy Pancakes MAKES 8 PANCAKES

What is it about pancakes? They are so simple and yet such a wonderful breakfast. I love surprising my kids on test days with a breakfast of pancakes, and every Halloween we make them the morning after trick-or-treating, filling them with chopped-up candies.

There's just something about a well-cooked pancake made from scratch. Look, I get it: there are a *million* premade pancake mixes, and in full disclosure, the odds of there being a box of one in my cupboard right now are very high. However, I always feel a bit special when I skip the premade stuff. I will sneak in a bit of extra vanilla for calm and relaxation, maybe a pinch of cinnamon to incite exploration and adventure, or some chocolate chips for, well, *all* the good things.

1 cup all-purpose flour, sifted

2 tablespoons sugar

1 tablespoon baking powder

Pinch salt

1 egg, beaten and room temperature

¾ cup and 2 tablespoons milk, lukewarm

2 tablespoons unsalted butter, melted and cooled

2 teaspoons vanilla extract

Cooking oil (vegetable oil or olive oil) or cooking spray

**1.** In a medium bowl, combine all your dry ingredients: flour, sugar, baking powder, and salt.

**2.** In a separate bowl, mix together your wet ingredients: the egg, milk, melted butter, and vanilla. Be careful to let the butter cool before adding it to the bowl so as not to cook your eggs.

**3.** Pour the wet mixture into the dry mixture and stir well. The perfect batter will look far from perfect; lumps, even a few streaks of flour are all acceptable. Usually 20 to 30 seconds of gentle stirring is perfect. The batter's consistency at this point should resemble a slightly thick, lumpy cake batter.

**4.** Set the batter aside for 5 to 10 minutes. This will help it "relax," and quite a few of the lumps will disappear. You can even leave this overnight (preparing it up to 2 days ahead!) in your refrigerator—but make sure you do not add the baking powder until right before you make the pancakes.

**5.** Heat a heavy-bottomed nonstick pan over medium-low heat and coat it with cooking oil. Working in batches, use a 1/4-cup measure to scoop and drop the batter into the pan so that you get evenly sized pancakes. *Expect that first pancake to be a bit of a tester: a chance to get the sense of how things can, and then should, go. We don't always get a chance to run a quick test before we jump, so take this small victory and enjoy the ability to pivot, adjust, and keep going. Remember how helpful, how empowering that initial experiment feels, no matter how small or even how poorly it may turn out. Make room for more chances to give yourself permission to experiment, explore, and pivot to craft exactly what you want in this moment and beyond.*

**6.** Cook until the top surface forms bubbles (about 1 minute or so), and then carefully (so as not to burst any air that may have formed inside) flip and cook for a minute or so on the other side. Adjust the heat and add additional cooking oil as needed.

**7.** Ideally serve while still hot. Straight from the pan to the plate! However, if you'd like to eat with everyone together, place on a baking sheet in a preheated 200°F oven to keep warm. Try not to overlap or stack the pancakes, as that can make them soggy rather than fluffy. And we are totally making fluffy pancakes today!

*Tip*

................................

If you want super fluffy pancakes, separate your egg yolk from the white and add in the yolk when you combine the wet ingredients, but reserve the white. Right before cooking, fold in your egg white.

# Simple Sunday Waffles MAKES 4 TO 6 LARGE WAFFLES

I named these waffles after Sundays, but really they are for any morning absent of the trill of an alarm clock, the nagging obligation of a calendar event, or a list of urgent errands or chores. Or, at least, any morning you're willing to ignore all of these things in favor of lovely fluffy waffles topped with warm, almost-melted butter and drizzled in delicious New England maple syrup.

The cheese added doesn't just provide perfectly light waffles but will transform what can often be a time of day defined by chaos. Along with the sugar and vanilla, it will concoct for you the kind of soothing, love-filled restorative that is just right for a quiet morning.

For the toppings, we love piling on melted butter and maple syrup, or even peanut butter and banana slices with syrup. When your favorite berries are in season, a scoop of them and some whipped cream is fantastic too!

1 ½ cups all-purpose flour

2 teaspoons baking powder

½ teaspoon baking soda

½ teaspoon salt

2 tablespoons sugar

Zest of ½ lemon

¾ cup and 3 tablespoons milk

½ cup ricotta cheese

2 eggs

5 tablespoons and 1 teaspoon unsalted butter, melted

Juice of ½ lemon

1 teaspoon vanilla extract

Cooking spray

Toppings of choice for serving

**1.** In a medium bowl, whisk together the flour, baking powder, baking soda, and salt and set aside.

**2.** In a small bowl, combine the sugar and lemon zest, stirring with a fork until the sugar has a lovely lemon smell.

**3.** Whisk together the flour mixture and lemon sugar.

**4.** In a separate bowl, combine the milk, ricotta, eggs, butter, lemon juice, and vanilla.

**5.** Add the egg mixture to the flour mixture and stir until completely combined. *This is the perfect moment to accept some imperfection–the batter is actually better with a few lumps (so don't overmix it). We often forget that moments of imperfection, when we fail to make something beyond reproach, have beauty in them. Sometimes we need a few flaws to make something truly great–or, in this case, delicious.*

**6.** Let the batter rest for a bit; this can be 15 minutes or overnight in your refrigerator.

**7.** Heat the waffle iron as you normally would, spraying lightly with cooking spray.

**8.** Spread 1/4 cup of batter into the waffle iron for each waffle and cook until golden brown.

**9.** Either serve immediately with your preferred topping and eat the waffles right away, or wrap them tightly in plastic wrap and freeze to save them for a weekday treat warmed up in the toaster or oven.

lemon

rejuvenation

# Savory Waffles  MAKES 4 TO 6 LARGE WAFFLES

These waffles are perfect for picnics, road trips, and school lunches. When the kids were small I would make these ahead of time and then cut them into strips and serve them with dip. Full disclosure: I still do this for myself.

1 ½ cups all-purpose flour

2 teaspoons baking powder

½ teaspoon baking soda

½ teaspoon salt

2 tablespoons sugar

Zest of ½ lemon

2 eggs

¾ cup and 3 tablespoons
   milk

5 tablespoons and 1
   teaspoon unsalted butter,
   melted

¼ cup ricotta cheese

¼ cup sour cream

Juice of ½ lemon

1 teaspoon vanilla extract

Cooking spray

*Ingredients continued on*

*page 31*

**POTENTIAL ADD-INS**

**HERBS, CHEESE, AND CHIVES**

*Aids in remembrance, eases grief, empowers*

1 teaspoon garlic salt

1 teaspoon dried parsley

½ teaspoon dried rosemary

¼ teaspoon dried tarragon

1 ½ cups shredded smoked Gouda cheese

½ tablespoon chives

**SWISS AND TURKEY**

*Infinite, universal, greatness in small steps*

¾ cup shredded Swiss cheese

¾ cup shredded extra-sharp cheddar cheese

½ cup chopped turkey

1 shallot, finely diced

1 teaspoon mustard powder

**BACON AND CHEDDAR**

*Adaptability, luck*

6 ounces bacon, cooked until crisp and then crumbled

¾ cup grated cheddar cheese

6 green onions, white and light-green parts only, thinly sliced

## CHICKEN AND PEPPERS

*Uncovers problems,*
*encourages love,*
*protects*

¾ cup shredded
rotisserie chicken

1 red or green bell
pepper, finely diced

1 red onion,
finely diced

1 teaspoon smoked paprika

## POTENTIAL DIPS FOR SERVING (OPTIONAL)

Honey Mustard
(see page 284)

BBQ Sauce
(see page 283)

Chipotle Mayo
(see page 282)

Maple syrup, for a sweet
contrast

**1.** In a medium bowl, whisk together the flour, baking powder, baking soda, and salt and set aside.

**2.** In a small bowl, combine the sugar and lemon zest, stirring with a fork until the sugar has a lovely lemon smell.

**3.** Whisk together the flour mixture and lemon sugar.

**4.** In a separate bowl, combine the eggs, milk, butter, ricotta, sour cream, lemon juice, and vanilla.

**5.** Add the egg mixture to the flour mixture and stir until completely combined. Be careful not to overmix the batter.

**6.** Let the better rest for a bit; this can be 15 minutes or overnight in your refrigerator.

**7.** Heat the waffle iron as you normally would, spraying lightly with cooking spray. As the waffle iron heats, fold in the add-ins of your choice.

**8.** Spread 1/4 cup of batter into the waffle iron for each waffle and cook until golden brown.

**9.** Serve waffles immediately or store individually tightly wrapped and frozen. We cut these in strips and dip them in honey mustard, BBQ sauce, or any other delicious dip. If frozen, they are great heated up in the toaster or oven.

# Sugared Lemon Waffles MAKES 4 TO 6 LARGE WAFFLES

These are a wonderful embodiment of summer and brightness. A sweet start to the day, a welcome of the morning, they bring revitalization and luck and, when topped with berries, will fill you up with love.

3 tablespoons sugar

Zest of 3 fresh lemons

1 ½ cups all-purpose flour

2 teaspoons baking powder

½ teaspoon baking soda

½ teaspoon salt

¾ cup and 1 tablespoon
   milk

½ cup ricotta cheese

5 tablespoons and 1
   teaspoon unsalted butter,
   melted

2 eggs

6 tablespoons lemon juice

1 tablespoon vanilla extract

Cooking spray (optional)

Fruit, syrup, whipped cream,
   or other toppings of
   choice, for serving

**1.** In a small bowl, combine the sugar and lemon zest, stirring together with a fork until well combined. Set aside. This makes one of my very favorite scents and is the perfect way to start a weekend morning.

**2.** In a larger bowl, whisk together the flour, baking powder, baking soda, and salt.

**3.** Add your lemon sugar to the larger bowl of dry ingredients.

**4.** Combine the milk, ricotta, butter, eggs, lemon juice, and vanilla in a separate bowl or large cup. (I like to use a large liquid measuring cup.)

**5.** Once the wet ingredients are well combined, add them to the bowl with the dry ingredients and mix well. Resist overmixing—it's okay if there are a few lumps in your batter. Imperfect, delicious-smelling batter is what we're after.

**6.** Let the batter rest for a bit; this can be 15 minutes or overnight in your refrigerator.

**7.** Preheat your waffle iron according to its instructions. Lightly spray with cooking spray if needed.

**8.** Drop about 1/4 cup of batter into the iron for each waffle. Cook until slightly crispy on the edges.

**9.** Serve immediately with your favorite toppings. We like our waffles completely indulgent with strawberries, strawberry syrup, whipped cream, and lemon zest, but they are equally good topped with vanilla yogurt, fresh berries, and granola.

# Dutch Baby (German Pancake) MAKES 1 PANCAKE

Dutch baby pancakes are the ultimate breakfast adventure and a perfect treat to make during a waxing moon as their beautifully round golden rise mimics the growing moon—though if I'm honest, they're a perfect way to celebrate the rising sun any morning. Make this on days you need a small reminder that there's always room to bring more light to your day, and you are ready to rise and meet it.

This pancake is super simple to make but feels adventurous and celebratory every time you take it out of the oven. The anticipation and excitement of watching it slowly grow up above the pan never gets old. It is a reminder that surprise and delight don't have to be reserved for holidays.

½ cup all-purpose flour

2 tablespoons sugar

¼ teaspoon kosher salt

½ cup whole or 2 percent milk

2 eggs

2 tablespoons vanilla extract

2 tablespoons unsalted butter, plus more as needed

**FOR SERVING (OPTIONAL)**

Powdered sugar

Maple syrup

Jam of choice

Fruit of choice

**1.** Place the flour, sugar, salt, milk, eggs, and vanilla in a blender or food processor fitted with a blade attachment. Blend for 10 seconds, scrape down the sides, and then blend for another 10 seconds. You want to make sure everything is completely combined. The batter will be quite loose and liquidy, so don't worry if it doesn't feel like a normal pancake batter—you're good!

**2.** Set the batter aside to rest for 25 minutes.

**3.** Place a 9- to 10-inch ovenproof skillet or 9-by-13-inch pan with 1- to 2-inch-high edges on the middle rack of your oven, making sure to remove any racks above it. Heat the oven to 425°F, keeping the pan inside so it will be hot when you need it. The pan should be in the heating oven for 10 to 15 minutes, long enough for the oven to come to temperature and the pan to get hot.

LIGHT, FIRE, AND ABUNDANCE

**4.** Once the pan is hot, remove it from the oven and place it on a safe, heatproof surface nearby.

**5.** Place 2 tablespoons butter in the pan and swirl to melt the butter and coat the bottom and sides of the pan. If needed, take a separate stick of butter and run it over the sides of the pan.

**6.** Pour the batter into the pan and then place the pan into the oven while swirling it slightly to make sure it is coated evenly on all sides.

**7.** Bake until the Dutch baby is puffed, lightly browned across the top, and darker brown on the sides and edges, 15 to 20 minutes. *It's so much fun to watch rise, so if you have an oven window and light, take advantage! If not, try not to open the oven to check on the progress, as you want to keep the temperature steady as it rises. In this case you will have to just trust yourself, trust the pan, trust the oven, trust all the things. This is not something I'm particularly good at, but doing so provides excellent practice with a delicious reward at the end.*

**8.** You can either serve from the pan or transfer the Dutch baby to a serving platter or cutting board. Dust with powdered sugar, top with any other toppings of choice, and cut into wedges.

*Tip*

If you'd like to put fruit in your Dutch baby and not just on top, arrange the fruit in the bottom of the skillet before you pour the batter in. If you place the fruit on top, it won't rise as high. We like to add chocolate chips from time to time, but fair warning- they can make the skillet hard to clean!

# Samaire's Strawberry Scones

MAKES 16 SMALL SCONES

One of the first recipes Samaire made all by herself, these scones are a delicious snack-size treat. They're soft and sweet with a touch of sour to keep you on your toes, much like my daughter herself. We all adore these, and coupled with a nice cup of tea, they can make for a wonderful afternoon respite.

2 cups all-purpose flour, and more for flouring the work surface

⅓ cup sugar

2 teaspoons baking powder

¼ teaspoon baking soda

¼ teaspoon salt

½ cup (1 stick) unsalted butter, frozen

1 cup chopped strawberries

½ cup and 2 tablespoons heavy cream

1 ½ cups powdered sugar

½ teaspoon lemon zest

3 tablespoons lemon juice

½ teaspoon vanilla extract

**1.** Line a baking sheet with parchment paper.

**2.** In a large bowl, stir together the flour, sugar, baking powder, baking soda, and salt.

**3.** Grate the frozen butter into the bowl of dry ingredients. When you get to the end of the butter, chop it into small pieces with a knife.

**4.** Stir in the strawberries, coating them completely with the flour mixture, then slowly pour in the heavy cream.

**5.** Carefully bring the dough together with a wooden spoon or Danish dough whisk and then with your hands. Starting with the spoon or whisk limits the time the dough is exposed to the heat from your hands. Work the dough as little as possible, bringing it together by kneading gently. (The less you work the dough, the less the butter melts and the better your scones will be!)

**6.** Place the dough on a lightly floured surface and press it into a 1/4-inch-thick rectangle. Cut the rectangle into four sections, then cut each section twice diagonally to form four small triangles.

*If you'd like, take the triangles and curl them just slightly into crescent shapes, or form others into small balls, and these treats can resemble phases of the moon–a wonderful reminder to love ourselves in all our phases, for they each have their own sweetness.*

**7.** Place each scone on the baking sheet, leaving 1 inch of space between them.

**8.** Place the baking sheet in the freezer for approximately 20 minutes to cool the dough. Meanwhile, preheat your oven to 350°F.

**9.** Place the sheet in the preheated oven for 20 minutes, then remove and let cool.

**10.** Combine the powdered sugar, lemon zest, lemon juice, and vanilla, stirring together with a fork or a whisk until smooth.

**11.** Drizzle the lemon-sugar mixture over the scones and serve.

# Crepes MAKES 6 CREPES

Crepes are another item that can feel so fancy they seem too intimidating to make. In reality, they are just super thin pancakes, but having them for a meal—whether filled with sweet or savory items, or even stacked with pastry cream between—feels utterly indulgent. Let go of perfection and enjoy the process of slowly tilting your pan and watching the batter spread and cook, creating one wonderful treat at a time.

4 eggs

2 ¼ cups milk, room
   temperature

6 tablespoons unsalted
   butter, melted, and more
   to coat the pan

2 cups all-purpose flour

Pinch salt

*Ingredients continued on
   page 42*

**1.** In a blender or small food processor, combine all ingredients and pulse for 10 seconds.

**2.** Place the crepe batter in the refrigerator for at least 1 hour. This allows the bubbles to subside so the crepes will be less likely to tear during cooking. (The batter will keep for up to 48 hours, making this a great make-the-night-before breakfast!)

**3.** Place a small (8- to 9-inch) nonstick or cast-iron pan over medium to medium-high heat to preheat. You will want it hot for the crepes.

**4.** Melt a little butter in the bottom of the pan and swirl to coat.

**5.** With the hot skillet in one hand, use your other hand to pour 1/4 cup of the crepe batter slowly and steadily into the center of the pan, tilting the skillet around to spread the batter evenly in a very thin layer. Like most things, this gets easier with practice.

**6.** Cook for 30 seconds and then flip. These won't flip like pancakes, so I often use an offset icing spatula or even a butter knife. Anything that will help lift it gently up so you can turn it over.

## FOR SWEET CREPES ADD:

1 tablespoon sugar

1 teaspoon vanilla extract

For serving: strawberries, bananas, hazelnut spread (such as Nutella), or other sweet filling of choice

## FOR SAVORY CREPES ADD:

1 tablespoon minced fresh herbs of choice (parsley, chives, etc.)

## FOR SERVING

Cooked eggs, thinly sliced ham, Swiss cheese, or other filling of choice

**7.** Cook for another 10 seconds, then place the crepe on a large cutting board or baking sheet, being careful not to overlap them as you lay them flat to cool.

**8.** Continue until all the batter has been used.

**9.** After the crepes have cooled, you can stack them and store them in resealable plastic bags in the refrigerator for several days.

**10.** When ready to fill and serve, you have options for how to proceed. One option is to place a thin layer of filling across the whole of each crepe and then roll them up to form jellyroll-like cylinders. Our favorite way to fold our crepes is to place filling on half of each crepe, then fold them over into a half-moon or half-circle and add more filling on just half of that (a quarter of the whole original circle) and then fold again so the crepe forms a point at one end. Top each with whipped cream or any extra filling of your choice and enjoy!

# Monkey Milk MAKES 1 SMOOTHIE

Creating a meaningful moment over a meal or snack doesn't have to be complicated. When my son, Wylie—my silly little monkey—was small, we would make this smoothie together, him on my hip, dropping in the banana and pinching the cinnamon. It was our small ritual to help us get ready for school and work, a small spell of sorts to ease our hearts in the days daycare drop-offs were filled with tears. I remember thinking that someday it wouldn't be so hard to leave him, that the absence in my heart would lessen as we both grew a bit. I'm not sure it has lessened as much as I've grown into it, but we still enjoy making our Monkey Milk together, even if only one of us now needs that moment.

The smoothie is quick enough to put together with ingredients easily on hand. Its recipe is a simple prayer, with cinnamon to help him carry my love with him through the day, and bananas for encouragement so he might have resilience as he faces his own adventures, until we reunite and I can once again hold him close.

1 cup ice
½ cup milk
½ banana
1 teaspoon cinnamon
  powder

**1.** Place ice, milk, banana, and cinnamon in a blender and combine, making sure ice is thoroughly crushed.
**2.** Pour into a glass and serve, preferably with a brightly colored straw.

LIGHT, FIRE, AND ABUNDANCE

# Breakfast Biscuit Balls MAKES 24 PALM-SIZE BISCUIT BALLS

These aren't the prettiest of breakfast items, but to be honest, they are one of our favorites. These biscuit balls are easy to fix ahead of time to have breakfast (or really any meal) ready to go for the rest of the week, customized with your favorite ingredients. Add in some scrambled eggs and peppers for a Western-style biscuit that is a token of life and luck, or keep as is for a small snack ready to protect and give courage. Regardless, these won't last long—at least, they rarely do in our house.

1 pound ground spicy
   Italian sausage

2 cups shredded cheddar
   cheese

1 ½ cups Homemade
   Baking Mix (see page 46)

¼ cup chopped green
   onions

¼ cup heavy cream

1 teaspoon onion granules

1 teaspoon Italian seasoning

1 teaspoon garlic powder

Black pepper, to taste

**1.** Preheat your oven to 325°F. Line a baking sheet with parchment paper.

**2.** Combine all ingredients in a large bowl. You can use a large wooden spoon to combine, but I find using my hands works best. *There's something about hand-kneading dough that can pull you straight into the moment like few other things. So dig in and revel. Take notice of your innate magic in this process—of being able to take disparate items and combine them into something new with nothing but your hands. It's no small thing. You are no small thing.*

**3.** Use a small cookie scoop or spoon to roll 1-inch balls of dough and place on the baking sheet, making sure to leave a couple inches of space between each.

**4.** Bake for 15 to 20 minutes, until golden brown and cooked through.

# Homemade Baking Mix MAKES 7 CUPS

We all have enough going on without feeling like everything has to be made from scratch all the time to have meaning. Who has time for that? I find having mixes and various shortcuts on hand to ease the time and effort it takes to get certain foods ready to eat can be a lifesaver. This one is hands down one of my favorites. It is an alternative to products like Bisquick and the perfect secret weapon to keep in the cupboard or fridge, ready to make any number of delicious snacks and meals.

6 cups all-purpose flour

3 tablespoons baking
  powder

1 tablespoon salt

1 cup (2 sticks) unsalted
  butter, cold and cubed,
  or 1 cup vegetable
  shortening, cold and
  cubed

**1.** Combine the flour, baking powder, and salt in a food processor and pulse for about 20 seconds, or whisk thoroughly by hand.

**2.** Add the butter or vegetable shortening and pulse in the food processor, or use a pastry cutter or fork to mix until the cubes are broken and the mixture becomes consistently sandy, like crumbs, cornmeal, or grated Parmesan.

**3.** Place the baking mix into an airtight container and store in the refrigerator for up to 3 months. You can also make a big batch and freeze it, but be sure to bring the amount you need to room temperature before using it.

# Quick Drop Biscuits MAKES 12 BISCUITS

1 ½ cups Homemade

Baking Mix

(see page 46)

½ cup milk

**1.** Preheat your oven to 450°F.

**2.** In a large bowl, stir together the baking mix and milk.

**3.** Scoop heaping tablespoons full of dough and drop them onto an ungreased baking sheet.

**4.** Bake for 8 to 10 minutes, or until golden brown.

# Easy Pancakes MAKES 12 PANCAKES

1 cup milk

2 eggs

1 teaspoon vanilla extract

2 cups Homemade Baking
  Mix (see page 46)

1 tablespoon sugar
  (optional)

4 tablespoons unsalted
  butter, melted, and more
  to coat the pan (you can
  also use cooking spray)

**1.** In a large bowl, stir the milk, eggs, and vanilla together until well blended.

**2.** Add the baking mix and sugar, then let the batter rest for 5 to 10 minutes in a cool place.

**3.** Preheat a griddle or skillet and grease with butter or cooking spray. Working in batches, pour the batter 1/4 cup at a time onto the hot griddle or skillet.

**4.** Cook approximately 1 minute, until the pancakes start to bubble, and then flip and cook until done. The bubbles are key to have before you flip; they will start in earnest at the edges, and when you start to see a few in the center, you should flip the pancake over.

**5.** Repeat with the remaining batter.

vanilla          soothing

# Savory Breakfast Bake SERVES 8

I almost hate to call this a recipe. It is more of a guide or suggestion at best. Use the bread, eggs, and milk as a base and then fill with your favorite vegetables, meats, and spices. You could even replace the Tater Tots with hash browns, add in tomatoes, and use mozzarella—make this delicious in a way only you can.

This is super easy to make the night before and bake as everyone wakes up, but it works just as well sitting in the fridge for only an hour or so before being served for brunch. Either way, it's a lovely way to start your day.

½ pound sweet Italian
  sausage

½ pound hot Italian sausage

5 slices bacon

6 ounces Tater Tots

Olive oil or cooking spray

6 ounces brioche (or Italian
  bread or other bread of
  choice), cut into ½-inch
  cubes

¾ cup shredded cheddar
  cheese, divided

½ cup shredded Gruyère
  cheese, divided

1 green bell pepper, diced

1 red bell pepper, diced

5 white button mushrooms,
  chopped

*Ingredients continued on*
  *page 51*

**1.** In a medium skillet, brown the sausages and fry the bacon and then drain the fat from the meat. Break the sausages up and dice the bacon into bite-size pieces.

**2.** Cook the Tater Tots according to package directions, then set them aside to cool.

**3.** Lightly grease the bottom of a 9-by-13-inch baking pan with the oil.

**4.** Place the bread cubes across the bottom of the pan.

**5.** Reserve a few pieces of the browned meat and place the rest in a layer over the bread along with 1/2 cup of the cheddar and 1/4 cup of the Gruyère. Reserve a few of the pepper and mushroom pieces and spread the rest over the cheese, then top with the cooled Tater Tots. Set the reserved cheese, meat, and vegetables aside for garnish. *It's always nice when making a casserole or similar dish to reserve a bit of filling for the top to let people know what they are about to eat—not to mention it can look attractive as well.*

8 eggs

2 ⅔ cups whole milk

1 tablespoon chopped fresh
  parsley

1 tablespoon onion
  granules

¾ tablespoon garlic powder

1 ½ teaspoons kosher salt

½ teaspoon black pepper

¼ tablespoon smoked
  paprika

**6.** Combine all the remaining ingredients in a large mixing bowl and whisk well.

**7.** Pour the mixture over the bread and meat and use a wooden spoon or your favorite flat-sided utensil to push any dry bread below the mixture.

**8.** Sprinkle the top with the remaining 1/4 cup of each cheese and garnish with the reserved vegetable and meat pieces.

**9.** Cover with foil and refrigerate overnight. *(Now, if you're anything like me you will forget about this part and want to use this right away. I can't help with that, but I can say I've forgotten to plan for this step and only refrigerated for 1 hour and it's been fine. Nothing catastrophic has happened; everything still cooks and is A-OK. But I highly recommend making it the night before, if only to make space for what tomorrow might bring, let go of the day you have had, and give yourself something special to look forward to the next morning. We all deserve that.)*

**10.** Remove the casserole from the refrigerator and allow it to come to room temperature as you preheat your oven to 350°F.

**11.** Bake uncovered for 50 to 60 minutes. A toothpick placed in the center should come out clean when it is finished.

# Baked Blueberry French Toast SERVES 8

An excellent breakfast on the morning of a new adventure, be it school, work, or otherwise, this delicious and decadent blueberry dish can calm your nerves and help you accept changes ahead. Even better, the warmth of the cinnamon is a great reminder of love and that nothing is faced alone.

4 tablespoons unsalted
  butter or cooking spray

12 slices challah, cut into
  1-inch cubes

8 ounces cream cheese, cut
  into 1-inch cubes

1 pint blueberries, diced

12 eggs, beaten

2 cups milk

⅓ cup and 2 tablespoons
  maple syrup

2 tablespoons vanilla extract

½ packed cup brown sugar

2 tablespoons cornstarch

1 tablespoon cinnamon
  powder

**TOPPINGS
(OPTIONAL)**

Maple syrup

Powdered sugar

Yogurt

Blueberries

**1.** Lightly grease a 9-by-13-inch baking dish with the butter or cooking spray.

**2.** Cover the bottom of the dish with about half the bread cubes, then distribute the cubes of cream cheese across them.

**3.** Sprinkle the blueberries over the cream cheese, and then top with the remaining bread cubes.

**4.** In a large bowl, mix the eggs, milk, maple syrup, vanilla, brown sugar, cornstarch, and cinnamon and blend until completely combined. Pour the egg mixture over the bread cubes and use a wooden spoon to make sure the bread is covered.

**5.** Cover and refrigerate for at least 1 hour, but it can just as easily sit overnight.

**6.** Remove the dish from the refrigerator about 30 minutes before baking and preheat your oven to 350°F.

**7.** Bake, covered, for 30 minutes. Uncover and continue baking for 15 to 20 minutes, until the center is firm and the surface is lightly browned.

**8.** Serve warm topped with maple syrup, powdered sugar, yogurt, or all three, and more blueberries.

# Leek Frittata SERVES 4

What is the difference between a frittata and a quiche? I've looked it up a thousand times and I am still unclear. Is it the crust? The way it's cooked? Either way, this couldn't be simpler to make. Leeks provide protection and strength to existing love, while the thyme and oregano can add clarity and success. Mix it all together and you have a meal to share with dear friends and loving partners. If you can work in a joke about there being a leak in the boat, pan, or skillet, bonus points to you, my friend.

3 medium Yukon gold
   potatoes

3 large leeks, white and
   light-green parts only

5 tablespoons unsalted
   butter, divided

2 tablespoons olive oil,
   divided

1 ½ teaspoons salt (kosher
   salt if you have it), divided

8 eggs

¼ cup 2 percent milk

Black pepper, to taste

3 ounces goat cheese,
   crumbled

1 teaspoon dried thyme

1 teaspoon dried oregano

*Ingredients continued on
   page 54*

**1.** Dice the potatoes into 1/2-inch cubes and place in a medium saucepan.

**2.** Cover the potatoes with salted water and bring to a boil. Boil the potatoes until tender, about 10 minutes. Drain and let cool.

**3.** Slice the leeks into 1/2-inch-thick disks, place them in a colander, and rinse well. Set aside on paper towels to dry off the excess water.

**4.** Preheat your oven to 350°F and place a rack in the center.

**5.** Heat 3 tablespoons of the butter and 1 tablespoon of the olive oil in a 10-inch ovenproof nonstick skillet set over medium-high heat. (I usually use cast-iron.)

**6.** Once the butter is melted, add the leeks and 1/2 teaspoon salt and cook, stirring, for about 3 minutes, then add the potatoes. Stir another 3 to 4 minutes, until the leeks are tender and browned.

**7.** Transfer to a plate or any medium-size flat surface. I often use a flexible cutting board. Spread into an even single layer and let cool. You don't want the leeks and potatoes to be too hot when you add them

## FOR SERVING

Hot sauce (optional)

Butter lettuce or arugula
  salad topped with
  Simple Salad Dressing
  (see page 287)

to the eggs, as that could cook the eggs prematurely.

**8.** In a large bowl, whisk the eggs and milk with the remaining 1 teaspoon salt and several grinds of pepper.

**9.** Fold the leeks, potatoes, goat cheese, thyme, and oregano into the egg mixture until well combined.

**10.** Heat the remaining 2 tablespoons butter and 1 tablespoon olive oil over medium-low heat in your skillet. When the butter has melted, add the egg mixture, using a wooden spoon to distribute the potatoes, leeks, and cheese evenly if necessary.

**11.** Cook on the stovetop until the egg mixture begins to set around the edges. This will take 4 to 5 minutes.

**12.** Slide a spatula around the edges to ensure they won't stick, then transfer the pan to the oven and continue to cook until the frittata is set in the center, another 3 to 5 minutes.

**13.** Remove the pan from the oven and let sit for 5 minutes.

**14.** Carefully slide the frittata onto a cutting board or serving plate and cut it into slices. Top with hot sauce if you like it spicy.

**15.** Serve warm or at room temperature with a butter lettuce or arugula salad topped with Simple Salad Dressing.

# Traditional Biscuits MAKES 8 BISCUITS

When we have breakfast out, one of us almost always orders a biscuit. There's something so wonderful about a warm biscuit topped with a healthy (or rather not so much) dollop of butter and strawberry jam, or a nice fried egg and sausage covered in melty cheese. Even better when you're home and can curl up and watch some cartoons with the day spread lovely before you.

    These are quick to put together with ingredients you probably already have on hand and take very little time to cook, so they're perfect for a surprise breakfast on a weekday or a nice replacement for rolls at dinner. If you find yourself without the buttermilk, just add 1 tablespoon white distilled vinegar or lemon juice to a measuring cup and then pour in milk until you have a full cup total.

2 cups all-purpose flour, and more for flouring the work surface

2 teaspoons baking powder

½ teaspoon baking soda

½ teaspoon kosher salt

½ cup (1 stick) unsalted butter, frozen

1 cup buttermilk

**1.** Preheat your oven to 450°F.

**2.** Whisk the flour, baking powder, baking soda, and salt together in a medium bowl and set aside.

**3.** Grate the frozen butter on the large holes of a box grater. When you get to the last bit, just chop it up with a knife. No need for perfection—the tips of your fingers are worth more than that!

**4.** Add the butter to the dry ingredients.

**5.** Use your fingers or a pastry cutter to cut the butter into the flour and break up any clumps. If using your hands, be quick and efficient in an effort to keep the butter from getting warm and starting to melt. *Biscuits are a crazy experiment in trusting yourself and the process. They aren't super complex, but they force us to pay attention and move quickly. The colder the butter stays, the more delicious the biscuits will be. So move quickly. Trust yourself. You've got this—this and all other things too.*

**6.** Pour in the buttermilk and stir with a wooden spoon or rubber spatula until the dough comes together and pulls from the sides of the bowl.

**7.** Place the dough on a lightly floured surface and gently pat it until it forms a roughly 1-inch-thick rectangle. Make sure not to make it too thin, erring on the thicker side.

**8.** Sprinkle the dough with a little flour, fold it in half from top to bottom, and then pat it back down into its original shape. Repeat with the folding and patting, folding from each side in a clockwise manner 8 times.

**9.** Once completely folded, the dough should be a little springy to the touch.

**10.** Using a 3-inch round cutter, the bottom of a glass, or a jar lid, cut the dough into 6 biscuits. (Or make square biscuits using a knife! *Stray from convention!*) Cut what you can the first time, then refold and pat down the extra dough and cut more.

**11.** Arrange the biscuits in a 10-inch cast-iron skillet so that the biscuits touch each other, but not the sides of the pan. You can also use a round cake pan or pie plate.

**12.** Place the biscuits in the oven and raise the oven temperature to 500°F. Bake until golden brown, about 15 minutes.

**13.** Remove the pan from the oven and immediately transfer the biscuits from the pan to a clean surface. Serve immediately.

# Cheddar Biscuits MAKES 9 BISCUITS

Just the phrase "cheddar biscuit" makes my mouth water, let alone the idea of covering such a biscuit in garlic butter. So, here we are. It's just waiting for us to make it happen. Maybe the protective ingredients here help make them so irresistible, but you know what? Sometimes something is just delicious and makes us happy. So go drop some spoonfuls, and spread some joy.

2 cups Homemade Baking Mix (see page 46)

¾ cup shredded sharp cheddar cheese

⅔ cup milk

1 ¼ teaspoons garlic powder, divided

⅛ teaspoon onion powder

⅛ teaspoon smoked paprika

½ cup (1 stick) unsalted butter, melted

1 tablespoon finely minced fresh parsley, or 1 teaspoon dried, if fresh is not available

**1.** Preheat your oven to 450°F.

**2.** In a medium bowl, combine the baking mix, cheddar, milk, 1/4 teaspoon of the garlic powder, the onion powder, and paprika with a spoon until just combined. (They will rise better if the dough isn't overworked.)

**3.** Drop generous spoonfuls onto an ungreased baking sheet. This should make approximately 9 biscuits.

**4.** Bake 6 to 8 minutes, until golden brown.

**5.** While the biscuits are baking, combine the melted butter and the remaining teaspoon of garlic powder.

**6.** Brush the butter mixture over the warm biscuits immediately upon removing them from the oven, then sprinkle with the parsley.

**7.** Serve warm.

# Black Pepper Biscuits with Ham

MAKES 6 BISCUITS

Breakfast? Dinner? The two are hard to delineate. I refuse to choose. These are good any time of day.

2 cups all-purpose flour, and more for flouring the work surface

1 tablespoon baking powder

½ teaspoon baking soda

1 teaspoon salt

1 tablespoon black pepper, and a dash for topping

¾ cup (1 ½ sticks) unsalted butter, frozen

1 cup grated smoked Gouda cheese or other cheese of choice

½ cup and 1 tablespoon whole milk, divided, or ½ cup milk and 1 tablespoon water

1 egg

Mustard, to taste, for serving

½ pound honey ham, thinly sliced

**1.** Preheat your oven to 400°F. Line a baking sheet with parchment paper and set it aside.

**2.** In a large bowl, mix together the flour, baking powder, baking soda, salt, and pepper.

**3.** Grate the frozen butter into the flour mixture. When you get to the end, chop the last pieces with a knife.

**4.** Fully incorporate the butter into the flour mixture with a pastry cutter, fork, or your hands.

**5.** Drop in the Gouda and stir to combine completely.

**6.** Pour 1/2 cup milk into the flour mixture, carefully stirring until just combined.

**7.** Lightly bring the dough together with your hands, squeezing and kneading gently until just combined.

**8.** Place the dough on a lightly floured surface and gently pat it until it forms a roughly 1-inch-thick rectangle. Make sure not to make it too thin, erring on the thicker side.

**9.** Using a 3-inch round cutter, the bottom of a glass, or a jar lid, cut the dough into 6 biscuits. Cut what you can out the first time, then refold and pat down the extra dough and cut more. My last biscuit is always a little messy, but still delicious!

**10.** In a small bowl, whisk together the remaining 1 tablespoon of milk with the egg, creating an egg wash.

**11.** Place the biscuits on the baking sheet and brush their tops with the egg wash, then sprinkle with black pepper.

**12.** Bake about 12 minutes, or until the biscuits are fluffy and lightly golden brown.

**13.** Cut each biscuit in half, lightly spreading mustard on one side and then filling with ham. Serve while the biscuits are still warm.

**14.** Cover leftovers tightly in plastic wrap. These should keep refrigerated for 1 to 2 days, but they are definitely (like all biscuits) best just after they're made.

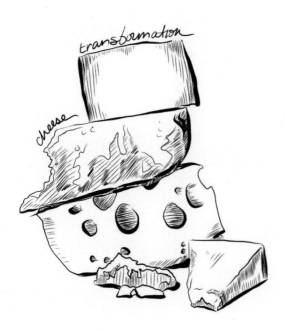

*Revel and Relish*

# MAIN DISHES

**THE WORD "DINNER" EVOKES** innumerable moments and meanings: televisions and tinfoil, dates and dancing. It's holidays around a crowded table and quiet moments over a simple plate. It's special and celebratory, ordinary and everyday. "Dinner" holds a multitude, just like us. And that's what the following recipes, I hope, contain: a little bit of celebration and a little bit of everyday—cause to pause and reflect, gather and laugh, and revel in all the in-betweens.

# Butter Crust Fish SERVES 4

The days can be long, and the challenges in them even longer. I have always seen the making of this meal in particular as a time to recalibrate. Let the day go and give yourself a minute (or twenty, or an hour) to forget about all that came before and not worry about what awaits tomorrow. Just be present. Just be. Spend a small moment concentrating on what you might need and might be able to give—to those you love and, yes, to yourself. This is a simple way to get there. Mix up the spices, press on the fish, and cook. Now go take a deep breath and pour yourself a calming drink.

½ cup (1 stick) and 2
tablespoons unsalted
butter, softened, and more
for greasing the pan
4 garlic cloves, minced
½ teaspoon onion powder
¼ teaspoon smoked
paprika
Pinch salt
Pinch black pepper
Four 6-ounce white fish
fillets (we often use cod)
1 cup crushed garlic
croutons (use your fave
bag of premade)

**1.** Preheat your oven to 425°F. Line a baking dish with parchment and lightly grease with butter.

**2.** In a medium bowl, use a fork to combine the butter, garlic, onion powder, and paprika. Add salt and pepper.

**3.** Place the fish fillets in the prepared baking dish. Scoop the butter mixture onto the top of the fish fillets. Then top with crushed croutons, pressing down into the fillets.

**4.** Bake for 15 minutes and then serve and enjoy!

# Crispy Chicken SERVES 4

I can't count the nights when I ask what sounds good for dinner and my son tells me, "Chicken." Specifically, a chicken sandwich. On those days, little else will suffice. So this was made for him. A little spicy, a lot delicious. The spices represent things that I hope for him: turmeric for energy and vitality, cayenne for removing any obstacle in his way, garlic to offer protection, and some onion to provide infinite possibility.

½ cup milk

1 teaspoon apple cider
   vinegar

2 eggs

1 ½ cups all-purpose flour

6 tablespoons plain or
   panko bread crumbs

1 tablespoon baking
   powder

1 tablespoon smoked
   paprika

1 tablespoon garlic powder

1 tablespoon onion powder

2 teaspoons turmeric
   powder

2 teaspoons salt

1 teaspoon black pepper

1 teaspoon cayenne
   powder

*Ingredients continued on*
   *page 66*

**1.** Heat the oven to 415°F (or if you have an old oven like mine, a little past the 400°F mark).

**2.** Place a metal rimmed baking sheet in the oven to heat up.

**3.** In a medium bowl, mix together the milk and apple cider vinegar. Then add your eggs and whisk well so they are thoroughly broken and combined with the milk. Set aside.

**4.** In a large bowl, cake pan, or pie plate, mix together the flour, bread crumbs, baking powder, paprika, garlic powder, onion powder, turmeric, salt, pepper, and cayenne.

**5.** Pat your chicken down with a paper towel to dry. Toss the chicken pieces in the flour mixture and coat evenly, shaking off any extra mixture. Set aside remaining flour mixture.

**6.** Dip the chicken pieces in the egg mixture.

**7.** Coat each piece with the flour mixture again, being super generous this second time. Press the mixture into the chicken with your fingers, making sure it sticks as well as possible.

2 pounds skinless, boneless chicken breast, cut into strips (2 to 3 strips per breast)

4 tablespoons unsalted butter or more as needed, cubed

*Tip*

......................................................

I love serving this with my homemade BBQ Sauce (see page 283), Honey Mustard (see page 284), or some Hot Honey (see page 267), with Broccoli Salad (see page 144) and Cheddar Biscuits (see page 57) as sides. My son, Wylie, will tell you it's best with a bit of hot sauce, a slice of cheddar cheese, and pickles on a potato bun.

**8.** Set each piece of chicken aside until all are coated, making sure not to layer or overlap them.

**9.** Take the baking pan out of the oven and drop the butter cubes across it. Tilt the pan and let the butter cover the whole bottom surface.

**10.** Place the coated chicken pieces on the tray, leaving space between them once again so the heat can move properly around them. You may need to bake them in two batches.

**11.** Bake 10 to 12 minutes, then carefully flip each piece of chicken, taking care not to knock the breading off. In a pinch I've used forks to help with the flip. While using them is not particularly graceful, they suit the times when I can't seem to get my spatula to bend to my will. Once flipped, bake another 10 minutes.

**12.** Let the chicken rest for a couple of minutes before serving. Any longer and it may get soggy. *I find the perfect timing by plating the sides and any other items, then plating the chicken. By the time the plates are assembled and we dig in, it's perfect.*

**13.** If you have leftovers, you can reheat them wonderfully by placing a wire rack over a foil-lined baking sheet and placing the leftover chicken on that. Set in an oven preheated to 425°F for 5 to 10 minutes.

# Baked Ranch Chicken SERVES 4

This recipe takes minutes to put together and is perfect for a busy weekday night. The creamy coolness of the ranch seasoning matches wonderfully with a peppery hot sauce, if you want to top it off as it comes out of the oven.

Cooking spray or olive oil

¾ cup bread crumbs

½ cup grated Parmesan cheese

2 tablespoons Homemade Ranch Dressing Powder (see page 68)

¼ teaspoon cayenne powder

½ cup mayonnaise (regular mayo or any flavor mayo will work–pick your favorite)

4 boneless, skinless chicken breasts

**Tip**

Serve with a salad of your choice, sweet potato fries, or some yummy macaroni and cheese!

**1.** Preheat your oven to 375°F.

**2.** Spray a 9-by-13-inch baking dish with cooking spray or wipe with a paper towel and olive oil.

**3.** On a shallow plate, combine the bread crumbs, Parmesan, ranch dressing mix, and cayenne.

**4.** Place the mayonnaise on a separate shallow plate.

**5.** Pat the chicken dry with a paper towel, then spread mayonnaise on each side, covering completely.

**6.** Once the chicken is covered, dredge it through the bread crumb mixture, patting it down with your fingers on each side to pick up as much of the bread crumb mixture as possible.

**7.** Place the coated chicken into your prepared baking dish.

**8.** Bake for 40 minutes. You will know it's done when a thermometer placed in the thickest section of each piece reads 165°F and the chicken is no longer pink in the middle. *I went years without a thermometer, so my chicken was regularly served with slices down the thickest part of it so I could see the color of the inside. This method of checking works too! Bonus: my kids assumed more times than not that I was being lovely and chopping pieces for them—and I was. Mostly.*

# Homemade Ranch Dressing Powder

MAKES 10 SERVINGS OF 2 TABLESPOONS EACH

1 cup dry buttermilk

2 ½ tablespoons dried
  parsley

2 tablespoons dried chives

2 ½ teaspoons garlic
  powder

2 teaspoons onion powder

2 teaspoons dried onion
  flakes

2 teaspoons dried dill

2 teaspoons kosher salt

½ teaspoon black pepper

½ teaspoon smoked
  paprika

¼ teaspoon cayenne
  powder

**1.** Combine all ingredients in a mixing bowl and whisk together.

**2.** Transfer the ranch mix to a jar or container that has a tight-fitting lid.

**3.** Store in the fridge for up to 2 months.

eases grief

parsley

# Sesame Noodles SERVES 6

This is a meal I can't make enough of. No matter whether I double or triple the recipe, it never seems to be enough. I love those kinds of recipes: the ones your family loves and you love making for them. This one's especially good for a family meal because it can be topped with everyone's favorite veggies and customized for taste. My daughter asks for this meal on the regular, topped with a perfectly (attempted, at least) fried egg. I am always happy to oblige.

3 tablespoons coconut aminos or low-sodium soy sauce

1 tablespoon toasted sesame oil

2 teaspoons red pepper flakes

½ cup and 2 tablespoons vegetable oil, divided

8 ounces roasted unsalted peanuts, finely chopped

Rinds of 3 oranges, sliced into thin strips

2 pounds ground chicken

Salt, to taste

Black pepper, to taste

20 ounces ramen noodles (4 "noodle bricks")

Ingredients continued on page 71

**1.** Mix the coconut aminos, sesame oil, and red pepper flakes in a heatproof bowl and set aside.

**2.** In a large skillet set over medium-high heat, combine 1/2 cup of the vegetable oil with the peanuts and orange rinds. Cook, stirring occasionally, until the peanuts are golden and the rinds look toasted, about 5 minutes.

**3.** Pour the contents of your skillet into the bowl with the red pepper flake mix and set aside.

**4.** Using the same skillet, heat the remaining 2 tablespoons of vegetable oil over medium-high heat and place the chicken in. You may have to do two batches, depending on the size of your skillet.

**5.** With a wooden spoon or similar utensil, spread and flatten the chicken along the bottom of the pan. Generously season the top with salt and black pepper.

**6.** Then let it be. No stirring, flipping, or separating for 5 to 7 minutes, until the chicken is turning a golden hue. *This can feel crazy uncomfortable–the not-doing-anything aspect when something is happening.*

## FOR SERVING (OPTIONAL)

Red pepper flakes

Shredded cabbage (purple is my favorite)

Shredded carrots

Diced peppers

Chopped peanuts

Fried onions

Fried eggs

*Often we are wired to stay busy, keep doing, and not take our eye off the ball! But right now, in this moment, give yourself permission to walk away. Not forever: I'll need you back in 5 to 7 minutes! But for now. Take a breath. Remind yourself that taking this moment to breathe won't hurt the overall process. You have done the work and you will return, but right now you get to fill your own cup. Literally, if you want. Get a nice cuppa. Treat yourself.*

**7.** When 5 to 7 minutes have passed, lift the chicken up a bit. It should be turning golden, and now is the time when you can flip it over. This flip never happens for me in one fell swoop. I inevitably break the chicken. And it's okay if you do too. Just make sure all the uncooked pieces are facing down on the hot skillet and let them cook through, which will take another 5 to 7 minutes. Then break up the chicken into small pieces and allow those to cook another 5 to 7 minutes.

**8.** Put a pot of water on to boil right after you turn the chicken, and prepare the ramen noodles according to package directions.

**9.** Toss your sauce with the noodles. Have some fun. Taste a few sample spoonfuls. Add a few more pinches of red pepper flakes if you want the dish spicier.

**10.** Grab some bowls and tongs if you have them (I always love to use tongs to move the noodles from the pot to the plate) and create decadent piles of delicious noodles. But wait, you're not done! Top with any combination of fresh crispy veggies, additional peanuts, crispy fried onions, and maybe even a fried egg per serving. *Enjoy.*

# Spicy Chili Noodles SERVES 6

These noodles are simple and leave room for you to add your favorite protein. (They go great with fried tofu, for example.) They are spicy, so taste as you go. You can always start with less of the red pepper flakes and add more later if you want. I love how this recipe can be a bit of a personality test. Will you dump all the garlic and pepper flakes in at once? Will you add more, assuming I've not indicated enough? Will you start small and increase as you go? Do what feels right. Bold or cautious, it will end up absolutely delicious.

16 ounces rice noodles or spaghetti

3 tablespoons vegetable oil

5 garlic cloves, minced

½ teaspoon grated or minced ginger, or more or less to taste

2 ½ tablespoons chili flakes, or more or less to taste

2 tablespoons balsamic vinegar

1 tablespoon dark soy sauce (regular is fine too)

½ teaspoon sugar

**FOR SERVING**

Sliced cucumber

Chopped green onion

Sesame seeds

Diced extra-firm tofu or sliced fried egg (optional)

**1.** Set a large pot on the stove and begin cooking the noodles according to the package directions.

**2.** Heat the vegetable oil in a small pot over medium heat. Add the garlic and ginger and sauté until fragrant, 30 seconds to 1 minute. *I like to balance the chili with the ginger in this dish; more chili flakes equals more ginger. So if you like your noodles spicy, consider increasing the ginger here.*

**3.** Remove the oil from the heat and mix in the rest of the ingredients for the noodles, adjusting the amount of chili flakes to your preferred heat level.

**4.** Toss the mixture with the noodles, reserving some of the mixture if you plan to add tofu.

**5.** Top with cucumber, green onion, and sesame seeds. You can also use diced extra-firm tofu or fried egg slices. If using tofu, make sure to toss it with the reserved sauce before adding it to the noodles.

# Peanut Noodles SERVES 6

Flavorful without being hot, these noodles hit the perfect spot between sweet and spicy. The ginger and carrots inspire confidence and a drive for authenticity; the peanut butter is a reminder of childhood pursuits. Serve this with an eye toward a new adventure and even more wonderful memories.

8 ounces spaghetti or other
  noodles of your choice

½ cup peanut butter

3 tablespoons water

3 tablespoons low-sodium soy sauce

2 tablespoons sesame oil

2 tablespoons rice vinegar

2 teaspoons brown sugar

1 garlic clove, minced

1 ½ teaspoons minced fresh ginger

¾ teaspoon sriracha

**FOR SERVING**

Crushed peanuts

Black sesame seeds

Sliced green onions

Shredded carrot

Shredded red cabbage

Green beans or other vegetable of
  choice, barely blanched, still crisp
  (optional)

Shredded rotisserie chicken (optional)

Tofu pieces (optional)

**1.** Cook spaghetti according to package instructions.

**2.** In a blender, combine the peanut butter, water, soy sauce, sesame oil, rice vinegar, brown sugar, garlic, ginger, and sriracha, blending until smooth.

**3.** Place the spaghetti into a large bowl and pour the peanut sauce on top. Use tongs to mix well.

**4.** Transfer the noodles to serving bowls and top with peanuts, black sesame seeds, and green onion slices. Add veggies, chicken, or tofu to taste.

# Wylie's Beef Stew SERVES 6

Every family has some sort of stew recipe, I imagine. The kind that uses up whatever is in the cupboards and provides some warmth when the weather starts to cool. It's the kind of recipe with a lot of clauses: "If you don't have this, use that." The making itself becomes the recipe after a while, cards and papers long ago left behind as each family cook adds their own spin to its creation. This is ours.

This recipe is a combination of bits and pieces of other recipes handed down through our families and is the first solid-food meal Wylie ever ate. It reminds me of home as it should be: warm and welcoming and rich in all the ways that matter. It also reminds me that time passes so very fast. It feels like just yesterday that Wylie was in his high chair, with all of us crowded around oohing and ahhing over this milestone. Time plays tricks, speeding up only to come to an abrupt stop. Making this stew lets me slow down a bit and reminds me it's okay to take all day to just revel in what we have.

10 garlic cloves, minced

2 tablespoons tomato paste

1 squeeze (a little more than
   1 teaspoon) anchovy paste

1 ½ cups all-purpose flour,
   or 2 cups if needed to
   thicken stew

4 teaspoons salt, or to taste

4 teaspoons black pepper,
   or to taste

*Ingredients continued on*
   *page 76*

**1.** In a small bowl, mix together the garlic, tomato paste, and anchovy paste and set aside.

**2.** Grab a large zip-top bag (or large bowl, if you're neater than I am) and pour in 1 1/2 cups flour and the salt and pepper. In a couple of batches, drop in the beef and cover thoroughly with the flour mixture. This will help create a thickening roux when you sear it in a moment. Set the beef cubes aside and dispose of the extra flour in the bowl or bag.

**3.** In a large heavy-bottomed pot with a lid available, heat the olive oil and melt your butter over medium-high heat.

OPPOSITE: WYLIE'S BEEF STEW WITH CHEDDAR MASHED POTATOES (SEE PAGE 154).

LIGHT, FIRE, AND ABUNDANCE

2 pounds stew beef (chuck
roast or similar), cubed

3 tablespoons extra-virgin
olive oil

3 tablespoons unsalted
butter

2 small red onions, sliced or
diced (about 1 ½ cups)

1 ½ cups beer (stout or
ale), or more if needed to
decrease stew's thickness

1 cup beef broth, or more if
needed to decrease stew's
thickness

2 tablespoons cumin
powder

4 dried bay leaves

12 small red potatoes (not
creamers!)

10 ounces frozen
sweet peas

**4.** Again in batches, place your beef cubes in the pot and cook to brown on all sides. Take care not to layer the beef or overcrowd the pot. I use tongs and let each side sit for 30 seconds to 1 minute, rotating each piece in turn and removing it from the heat once it's cooked. *As you're doing this, take a moment and breathe deeply. The repetitive process of slowly rotating the beef piece by piece presents the perfect time to let yourself relax. Feel the floor beneath you, the warmth in front of you. Think about the intention of this meal and what you wish to give or receive in its making and consumption.* Return all the beef to the pan if you have removed pieces.

**5.** Add the onions and let them begin to sweat and soften a bit, cooking for 2 to 3 minutes.

**6.** Add your tomato, garlic, and anchovy mixture and mix until fragrant. This won't take long, just 2 to 3 minutes. You'll want to be able to smell it all combining and have that moment of *yum*.

**7.** Slowly pour in your beer and scrape the bottom of the pan to make sure everything is getting incorporated.

**8.** Pour in your beef broth, then add the cumin and any additional salt and pepper to taste.

**9.** Drop in your bay leaves and bring the mixture to a simmer over medium heat. In 15 minutes, the stew should begin to thicken. If it doesn't look like it's thickening or you want it thicker, you can always add 1/2 cup flour. If it's starting to look too thick, pour in some more beer or broth, whichever your preference is.

Serve with Cheddar Mashed Potatoes (see page 154) and/or top with avocado, sour cream, or French onions—or use all of these. Do what makes you happy!

**10.** Add the potatoes and cover the pot. Let simmer for an additional 30 minutes, or until the potatoes pierce easily with a fork.

**11.** Add in your peas and simmer on the stovetop for 10 minutes.

**12.** Keep warm over low heat until you're ready to eat.

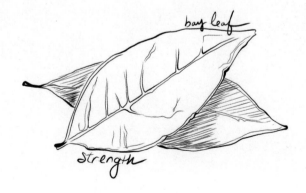

bay leaf

strength

# Curried Beef SERVES 4

This recipe is perfect for those months of shortened days and long nights—the time of year the world makes space for us to rest, plan, and prepare for the months ahead. Accordingly, this dish is topped with a cilantro purée, imbuing a sense of peace and calm. Here is a chance to review the work of the past year and decide what you want to do in the months and days ahead. This dish reminds us that when we put the initial work in, it's okay to step away and let it flow forth, let the result of our hard work happen, trusting our labors will enable our hopes to come to fruition.

2 tablespoons olive oil

2 pounds beef stew meat (chuck roast or similar), cubed

2 ½ tablespoons Madras curry powder

1 ½ teaspoons cumin powder

1 teaspoon salt, or more to taste

1 teaspoon black pepper, or more to taste

2 tablespoons unsalted butter

3 garlic cloves, minced

1 ½ tablespoons chopped or minced ginger

*Ingredients continued on*

*page 80*

**1.** Heat the oil in a heavy-bottomed pot set over medium-high heat.

**2.** Add the beef, working in batches if necessary, and sear the beef cubes on each side for 30 seconds to 1 minute. Be sure not to overcrowd the pan. Once seared, remove from the pot and set aside.

**3.** In a small bowl, combine the curry, cumin, salt, and pepper and set aside.

**4.** Melt the butter in the pot, add the garlic and ginger, and cook while stirring until fragrant, 3 to 4 minutes.

**5.** Add in the flour, whisking until well combined.

**6.** Return the beef cubes to the pot and cover thoroughly with the spice mixture. The beef should be evenly coated on each side.

**7.** Add the potatoes.

**8.** Crumble the slice of naan over the mixture, then add the tomatoes.

2 tablespoons all-purpose flour

10 small red potatoes
 (not creamers!), quartered

1 slice naan, and more for
 serving

28 ounces canned fire-
 roasted tomatoes

Cilantro Purée (see
 page 286), to taste

**9.** Let simmer for 25 to 30 minutes, or until the beef is cooked through and the potatoes are tender. If it is too heavy on the sauce, let simmer for 10 to 15 more minutes over low heat to thicken.

**10.** Serve with naan flatbreads and a generous spoonful of Cilantro Purée per serving.

protects against thievery

cumin

# Chicken Corn Chowder SERVES 6

When I was first learning to cook, this was my first chowder/soup/stew dish. I had never made anything like it before, but I wanted to use the bounty of corn that filled our local farmers market in Union Square for something special. This was the result—a pot full of delicious, homey, and rich flavors. The bacon adds a slight smoky flavor for the fall, while the corn brings a sweet, bright memory of the summer days that have just passed. This dish is perfect for one of those first crisp afternoons, and it is even better when served alongside a fresh Kale Apple Salad (see page 143).

4 cups chicken broth, divided

4 cups corn (fresh or canned), divided

3 slices bacon

1 ½ pounds boneless, skinless chicken breast, diced

1 white onion, chopped

2 teaspoons turmeric powder

½ teaspoon cayenne powder

1 large potato, peeled and diced

½ teaspoon salt

1 cup heavy cream

2 tablespoons chopped fresh parsley

⅛ teaspoon white pepper

**1.** Purée 1 cup chicken broth and 2 cups corn in a blender or food processor, then set aside.

**2.** Cook the bacon in a medium skillet over medium heat until crisp, then crumble it and set it aside. Reserve 2 tablespoons of the drippings.

**3.** Combine the 2 tablespoons of bacon drippings, the chicken, and onion in a heavy-bottomed pot. Cook, stirring frequently, for 10 to 15 minutes, until the chicken is cooked through and the onion pieces are translucent.

**4.** Add the turmeric and cayenne and stir for about 1 minute.

**5.** Add the puréed corn, remaining 3 cups broth, potato chunks, and salt to the pot.

**6.** Bring to a boil, then reduce the heat and simmer partially covered for 20 minutes, or until the potato is just tender.

**7.** Stir in the remaining 2 cups of corn, half the crumbled bacon, and the cream, parsley, and white pepper. Simmer for 2 to 3 minutes.

**8.** Remove from the heat and garnish with a sprinkle of the remaining crumbled bacon before serving.

# Chicken Carnitas SERVES 6

This is one of those recipes that have absolutely saved me on busy weeks. It's wonderful as a meal when surrounded with delicious vegetables, beans, and rice, but it can also be reincarnated in a multitude of delicious ways, such as cheesy baked tacos covered with dollops of guacamole, delicious nachos paired with peppery radishes, or even atop crisp, fresh lettuce with salsa and crumbled tortilla chips. You can't go wrong.

1 tablespoon vegetable oil

1 large white onion, chopped

8 garlic cloves, roughly chopped

1 tablespoon cumin powder

1 tablespoon dried cilantro

1 tablespoon chili powder

2 teaspoons kosher salt

½ teaspoon chipotle powder

¼ cup or one 4-ounce can diced green chili peppers

1 cup water

1 tablespoon low-sodium soy sauce

1 tablespoon apple cider vinegar

1 tablespoon dried oregano

3 pounds boneless, skinless chicken breast or thighs

*Ingredients continued on page 83*

**1.** Heat the oil in a heavy-bottomed pot or Dutch oven set over medium-high heat.

**2.** Add the onion and let sweat for about 2 minutes, and then add the garlic and sauté together until fragrant, 3 to 4 minutes. The garlic will begin to brown and the onion pieces will soften.

**3.** Add the cumin, cilantro, chili powder, salt, and chipotle powder and stir together for about 2 minutes.

**4.** Add the chili peppers, water, soy sauce, apple cider vinegar, and oregano. Stir to combine. *Think of the warmth that happens not just over a pot but over a meal made with love as you stir. As your spoon moves clockwise around the pot, bring that intention to this meal and state it aloud: "May it warm, may it fill, may those who eat it be nourished body and soul."*

**5.** Place the chicken in the pot. Try to submerge the meat as much as possible, but it's okay if the chicken isn't completely covered by the sauce.

**6.** Raise the heat to bring the sauce to a simmer, then cover and continue to simmer for 45 minutes.

**7.** Once the chicken is cooked (it will easily fall apart

**FOR SERVING
(CHOOSE 1)**

Rice and beans

Tortillas with your choice of
cheese

Tortilla chips

with a fork or reach an internal temperature of
165°F), take the lid off and shred with two forks.

**8.** Continue to simmer without the lid for another 5
to 10 minutes to let the extra liquid evaporate.

**9.** Serve in any myriad of ways: over rice and beans,
in tortillas with your choice of cheese as quesadillas,
on chips for some delicious nachos, or in Creamy
Chicken Enchiladas (see page 129)!

*Tip*
..............................

If you like crispy ends on
your carnitas, simmer until
all the extra liquid is gone
and then throw them in a
skillet over high heat, or
place them on a baking
sheet to broil.

# Spicy Lasagna SERVES 10

Multilayered and varied, lasagna is a way to remind ourselves of our own multitudes. We get caught up sometimes in the roles we are meant to play and the expectations that surround us, and we forget that we get to choose who we are in every moment. It's not always easy—and much like a beloved and well-known recipe, sometimes expectations corner us into places where our full selves aren't given the chance to shine, where we aren't left room to change and grow—but it starts with small moves forward. A small change here, an added ingredient there. Experiment not just with your food but with who you would like to be, who you would *love* to be. You are not just the roles you play and the expectations put upon you—you are part of an infinite universe with infinite possibilities and potential inside you. Maybe a good place to start is by spicing things up a bit, adding a bit of the unexpected.

1 pound broccoli

2 tablespoons olive oil

Salt, to taste

Black pepper, to taste

1 egg

15 ounces ricotta cheese

2 teaspoons dried parsley

½ teaspoon red pepper flakes

3 cups Spicy Arrabbiata Sauce (see page 271)

9 lasagna noodles

½ pound Asiago cheese, shredded

1 ¼ pounds Italian sausage

¼ cup chopped fresh parsley for garnishing

**1.** Preheat your oven to 400°F and line a rimmed baking sheet with parchment paper.

**2.** While the oven heats, clean the broccoli of its stems and chop the florets into bite-size pieces. Try to make them as similar in size as possible so they cook at the same rate.

**3.** Toss the broccoli florets with the olive oil and season with salt and pepper to taste.

**4.** Spread your florets in a single even layer on the baking sheet and place the sheet in the hot oven. Bake for 15 to 20 minutes, until the florets are browned and crisp around the edges, then remove and lower the oven temperature to 350°F.

**5.** In a small bowl, mix the egg, ricotta, dried parsley, red pepper flakes, and 1/4 teaspoon salt.

**6.** Spoon about 1 cup of Spicy Arrabbiata Sauce into the bottom of a 9-by-13-inch baking dish, then cover with three lasagna noodles, trimming the noodle sheets as needed to fit three per layer.

**7.** Layer half the ricotta mixture across the noodles and then sprinkle one-third of the Asiago across the entire top, followed by the roasted broccoli and one-third of the sausage. Cover with three more noodles, then top with the remaining ricotta mixture and another layer of the Asiago and sausage.

**8.** Cover with the last three noodles. Top with the remaining Spicy Arrabbiata Sauce followed by the rest of the sausage and then the Asiago.

**9.** Bake for 25 to 30 minutes, or until golden and bubbling.

**10.** Garnish with the fresh parsley and let stand for about 10 minutes before slicing and serving.

# White Lasagna SERVES 10

This recipe makes a meal that is rich, decadent, and a perfect experiment in smoothing the rough edges of your day. Release some of the pressures that hang over your shoulders, and celebrate with joy that you have made it through another day. Tomorrow will come soon enough, and it will be another chance to focus on the life that you are working so hard to perpetuate. Take comfort and build dinner tonight in the same way we reach the goals and dreams we have: one step, one layer at a time.

1 egg

15 ounces ricotta cheese

¼ cup chopped fresh
   oregano, and 2 teaspoons
   for garnishing

Heaping ¼ teaspoon salt

4 cups Pecorino Pepper
   Sauce (see page 280)

9 lasagna noodles

½ pound pecorino cheese,
   shredded

1 roasted rotisserie chicken,
   bones and skin removed,
   meat shredded

2 cups Spinach Walnut
   Pesto (see page 276)

¼ cup shredded mozzarella
   cheese

**1.** Preheat your oven to 350°F.

**2.** In a small bowl, mix the egg, ricotta, 1/4 cup oregano, and salt.

**3.** Spoon about 1 cup of the Pecorino Pepper Sauce into the bottom of a 9-by-13-inch baking dish, then cover with three lasagna noodles, trimming the noodles as needed to fit three per layer.

**4.** Layer half the ricotta mixture across the noodles, sprinkle one-third of the pecorino across the entire top, and then add a layer of half the chicken. Cover with three noodles and then another layer of the ricotta mixture and pecorino, along with all the pesto and the rest of the chicken.

**5.** Cover with the last three noodles.

**6.** Pour the remaining Pecorino Pepper Sauce on top of the noodles, followed by the remaining pecorino and the mozzarella, spreading each evenly.

**7.** Bake for 25 to 30 minutes, or until golden and bubbling.

**8.** Garnish with the remaining 2 teaspoons oregano and let stand for about 10 minutes before slicing and serving.

# Vegetable Lasagna SERVES 10

My first summer home from college, one of my best friends from high school brought a vegetable lasagna recipe back from his college to share with us. Chamoff had seemed to find himself that year we were apart in ways I was still struggling to unfurl. In my own heart, I was still pretty lost, and I clearly remember the afternoon he and I spent making a recipe similar to this one. The dish was filled to the brim with vegetables and absolutely delicious.

In full disclosure, I was *not* excited to eat it. The idea of a lasagna low in meat and high in greens did not appeal. But the afternoon we spent making it, with Chamoff telling me about how it came about and how his year had been, and me chopping and listening and just soaking up the presence of this friend I had so missed, is a memory I still treasure. He was not the same person I had known the years before. He was somehow amplified, and it filled my heart.

To my utter shock and surprise, I adored his lasagna too. This isn't his recipe, but I think of him every time I make it. Our lives diverged decades ago, not long after that afternoon, and I still miss him. But this lasagna always brings me memories of long summer afternoons and reunited friends, and of what it means to be brave enough to step out of what you know and to step into who you want to be. It reminds me of my friend Chamoff and his willingness to open up to an old friend and share a new piece of himself. May we all be so lucky to have friends like him and to find the bravery to grow and share with those we care about.

1 egg

15 ounces ricotta cheese

¼ cup chopped fresh
parsley

¼ teaspoon salt

3 cups Simple Marinara (see
page 270)

*Ingredients continued on
page 88*

**1.** Preheat your oven to 350°F.

**2.** In a small bowl, mix the egg, ricotta, parsley, and salt.

**3.** Spoon about 1 cup of marinara sauce into the bottom of a 9-by-13-inch baking dish, then cover with three lasagna noodles, trimming the noodles as needed to fit three per layer.

**4.** Layer half the ricotta mixture across the noodles and sprinkle one-third of the Parmesan across the

9 lasagna noodles

½ pound Parmesan cheese, shredded

2 zucchinis, diced

3 carrots, diced small

1 cup white button mushrooms or baby bella mushrooms, diced

1 green bell pepper, diced

¼ cup shredded mozzarella cheese

¼ cup chopped fresh basil for garnishing

entire top, then add all the zucchini and carrots, then 1/4 cup marinara sauce. Cover with three more noodles, then the remaining ricotta mixture and another one-third of the Parmesan, then add the mushrooms.

**5.** Cover with the last three noodles.

**6.** Top with the remaining marinara sauce, the green bell pepper, the rest of the Parmesan, and the mozzarella.

**7.** Bake for 25 to 30 minutes, or until golden and bubbling.

**8.** Garnish with fresh basil and let stand for about 10 minutes before slicing and serving.

prosperity

basil

# Traditional Chili SERVES 4 TO 6

Does anything epitomize the changing of the seasons into cooler weather more than a giant bowl of chili? From tailgates to office potlucks, chili appears every fall, ready to play. This is also one of those recipes that we all seemingly have stashed away somewhere: an uncle's secret tips, a grandmother's prized process, all ready to receive their much-deserved blue ribbon. This recipe is pretty simple yet altogether delicious—a great base on which to build your own award-deserving concoction.

2 tablespoons vegetable oil

1 pound ground bison or
  other ground meat of
  choice

Olive oil for cooking (if using
  bison)

1 red onion, diced into
  ¼-inch pieces

2 garlic cloves, minced

1 tablespoon dried oregano

1 tablespoon chili powder

1 teaspoon smoked paprika

1 teaspoon turmeric
  powder

1 teaspoon cumin powder

1 teaspoon onion powder

1 teaspoon garlic powder

*Ingredients continued on*
  *page 90*

**1.** Heat the vegetable oil in a heavy-bottomed pot set over medium heat until the oil glistens.

**2.** Add the meat and cook until browned, then remove the meat and set it aside. If you are using bison and there isn't much grease left in the pot, add enough olive oil to create 2 tablespoons of grease. If you are using a meat other than bison, there is likely plenty of grease still in the pot and you should drain all but 2 tablespoons.

**3.** Add the red onion and garlic to the pot and cook over moderately high heat while the onion softens, about 5 minutes, then add the meat back into the pot.

**4.** Lower the heat to medium, add all the herbs and spices, and cook until fragrant, about 1 minute.

**5.** Stir in the beans, tomatoes, and chicken broth and bring to a simmer.

**6.** Reduce the heat and continue to simmer the chili while it thickens, about 15 minutes. The lowered heat will keep it from burning and becoming bitter.

½ teaspoon cinnamon
  powder

Pinch cayenne powder, or
  to taste

15 ounces canned white
  beans or Northern beans,
  drained and rinsed

15 ounces canned pinto
  beans, drained and rinsed

15 ounces canned black
  beans, drained and rinsed

28 ounces canned diced
  tomatoes

2 cups low-sodium chicken
  broth

1 cup fresh or frozen corn
  (optional)

Kosher salt, to taste

Black pepper, to taste

**FOR SERVING**

Corn chips (such as Fritos)
  or other chips of choice

Shredded cheddar cheese

Jalapeños, seeded and
  diced into ¼-inch pieces

Chopped cilantro

Sour cream

**7.** Add the corn, if using. *This part is optional. I like the touch of sweetness corn contributes, a taste of the beautiful transition between summer and fall. The clear, crisp flavor speaks to the insight and divination it can provide–a presence of mind, a moment to stand still and look forward with clarity and assurance.*

**8.** Continue simmering on moderately low heat for another 10 to 15 minutes, until the chili has thickened to your desired consistency.

**9.** Season with salt and pepper and serve as desired. My family loves this most when served over corn chips with cheddar, jalapeños, cilantro, and sour cream.

# White Chili SERVES 4 TO 6

I love white chili. I love that it's a bit unexpected, a bit off track. It is both hearty and light, a weird magical amalgamation of chicken, beans, and spice—not what's expected, but almost always a welcome sight. It feels out of the ordinary, extraordinary even, and I hope when you make it, you feel that way too.

2 tablespoons olive oil

2 ½ tablespoons unsalted butter

1 white onion

5 garlic cloves

3 jalapeños, seeded and finely chopped

2 tablespoons all-purpose flour

1 teaspoon cumin powder

1 teaspoon dried oregano

½ teaspoon cayenne powder

2 cups chicken broth

3 chicken breasts, diced small

¼ cup or one 4-ounce can chopped green chili peppers

1 teaspoon salt, or more to taste

*Ingredients continued on page 92*

**1.** Warm the oil in a Dutch oven or heavy-bottomed pot set over medium heat, then add the butter, onion, garlic, and jalapeños and cook until the onions are soft and translucent, 2 to 3 minutes.

**2.** Stir in the flour to thicken, then add the cumin, oregano, and cayenne. Warm until fragrant, approximately 1 minute.

**3.** Add the chicken broth 1/4 cup at a time.

**4.** Add the chicken, green chilis, salt, and pepper.

**5.** Bring to a boil, then reduce the heat and simmer, covered, for 10 to 12 minutes, until the chicken is cooked through.

2 teaspoons black pepper,
or more to taste

31 ounces canned white
beans (two 15.5-ounce
cans)

10 ounces frozen corn

**FOR SERVING**

Shredded white cheddar
cheese

Diced red onion

Jalapeños, seeded and
finely chopped

Fresh cilantro

Tortilla chips

**6.** Add the white beans, corn, and more salt or pepper if desired. Bring back to a simmer and let cook another 10 minutes.

**7.** Keep warm on the stove until ready to serve. Before serving, top with white cheddar, red onion, jalapeño, cilantro, and tortilla chips broken into pieces.

northern beans

discovery & insight

# Cincinnati Chili SERVES 4 TO 6

Cincinnati chili is full of controversy. First off, no beans? What is this? And then there's the altogether inappropriate addition of chocolate *and* an overnight stay in the refrigerator. I know, I know. In the words of my teenage daughter, *"How dare you!"* Yet I do, I dare. Because my midwestern roots run deep, and Cincinnati chili has always been in my life. I am but one of generations carrying forth the torch, and what an interesting and yummy torch it is.

This chili is not meant to be scooped into bowls but instead dolloped over spaghetti or used to drench hot dogs. There's a particular way to layer the ingredients that I have never learned properly, but I will tell you this: this wackadoodle dinner is a fun one. Sweet and warm, spicy but not hot, it will throw you for a wonderful loop every time. And sometimes stepping a bit out of the norm is exactly what we need to see the world around us in a new way. Is this life-changing? Absolutely not. Is it different, intriguing, and perhaps the start of a great family debate? You betcha.

1 yellow onion

2 to 3 garlic cloves, minced

6 ounces tomato paste

1 ¼ pounds lean ground beef

2 cups water

2 teaspoons Worcestershire sauce

¼ cup chili powder

1 teaspoon brown sugar

1 teaspoon cinnamon powder

1 teaspoon garlic powder

*Ingredients continued on page 95*

**1.** Heat a large, heavy-bottomed pot or Dutch oven over medium-high heat.

**2.** Add the onion, minced garlic, and tomato paste to the dry pot and cook, constantly scraping the bottom with a wooden spoon, until the tomato smells rich and toasty. This should take 1 to 3 minutes.

**3.** Remove the pot from the heat and add the ground beef and water. Break the meat into fine pieces in the water using a potato masher or fork, then mix together into a sludge or slurry. *(I hate those words, but there you go. It's the best descriptor I could find. So, be warned—it will not look pretty, but press on. There's a method to this madness.)*

**4.** Add all the remaining chili ingredients except the apple cider vinegar and cocoa powder and mix well.

1 teaspoon cumin powder

¼ teaspoon allspice powder

¼ teaspoon ground cloves

¼ teaspoon red pepper
flakes, or more depending
on desired heat level

¾ teaspoon salt

⅛ teaspoon black pepper

2 tablespoons apple cider
vinegar

2 tablespoons unsweetened
cocoa powder

## FOR SERVING
## (OPTIONAL)

Cooked spaghetti

4 to 6 hot dogs (1 per
serving)

Grated cheddar cheese

Diced yellow onions

Red kidney beans

Oyster crackers

Hot sauce

**5.** Return the pot to low heat and simmer, uncovered, for 2 to 3 hours, stirring often. *Full disclosure: Just 1 hour of cook time will work, but letting the chili simmer for 2 to 3 hours is ideal, as it will reduce down properly and concentrate the taste. And who doesn't need nothing to do for a few hours while you "watch the chili"? Do what you need. Tell everyone you're busy making dinner, and enjoy a few blissful hours of whatever you want. I promise not to tell.*

**6.** Remove the pot from the stovetop and allow the chili to cool to room temperature. Once cooled, cover and store in the refrigerator overnight.

**7.** The next day, take out your chili and scrape as much fat off the top as possible.

**8.** Set the chili pot over medium-high heat and bring to a rapid simmer, then add the apple cider vinegar and cocoa powder.

**9.** Serve over spaghetti or on a hot dog with all your favorite toppings!

# Empanadas

There is something wonderful about the making of empanadas. Of course the eating of them is divine, don't get me wrong, but the making is where the real magic is.

A lot can be made ahead of time; in fact, all the parts and pieces are make-aheadable. (A new word! Use with abandon! Blame me.) So make it all ahead and then gather 'round the table with your kids, your friends, all the members of your family . . . and assemble these delicious pockets of delectable ingredients. Laugh, gossip, and tell stories. Share the perfect technique of stuffing and folding up these little pastries and experiment with new fillings.

But do it all together. Some of my favorite evenings have been standing in the kitchen next to my daughter, listening to whatever her favorite music is at the time, while we cup small circles of dough and scoop in bits of apples and chicken. We then pass the fork back and forth as we seal them up as best as we can, and eagerly wait to pull them from the oven to see our hard work come to fruition.

The sharing, the gathering, the collaboration on how to get them all *just right*, that's where the magic here lies. Enjoy it. Create space for it. Remember it for the gift it absolutely is.

Even if they come out a little lumpy, or with the filling spilling out a bit, it's still all wonderfully delicious.

**EMPANADA CRUSTS AND FILLING** MAKES 20 TO 25 SMALL EMPANADA CRUSTS

Let's be real: While I think homemade dough is sublime with empanadas, I also know that sometimes the magic comes from simply being able to get dinner on the table. So while you can make this recipe, it is by no means required for a delicious empanada experience. If you need to, grab some premade pizza dough or pie crust, or experiment with another premade dough. Just be sure if it's frozen you allow the time needed for it to thaw; frozen pizza dough can often take a few hours.

If you're feeling like the process of making your own could provide you with some time to be present and give you a chance to practice making some truly delicious crust, here are the deets. And it will keep overnight, so it's a great make-ahead item for a weekday meal.

3 ¼ cups all-purpose flour

1 tablespoon sugar

1 teaspoon salt

¾ cup (1 ½ sticks) unsalted
  butter, frozen

6 tablespoons vegetable
  shortening

⅔ cup ice water

1 egg, beaten

1 tablespoon milk

**FILLING OF CHOICE**

Apple Chicken Empanada
  Filling (see page 99)

Fajita Black Bean Empanada
  Filling (see page 100)

Potato Chorizo Empanada
  Filling (see page 101)

**1.** Combine the flour, sugar, and salt using a food processor fitted with a metal blade, or by hand using a whisk or fork.

**2.** Add the butter and shortening and pulse in the processor or mix with a pastry cutter or fork until the butter and shortening pieces are small and the ingredients become well combined and sandy.

**3.** Slowly add the ice water, then either use your hands to continue to combine the ingredients or pulse in the processor until the dough comes together.

**4.** Remove the dough from the bowl and pat it into a disk shape. Wrap it with plastic wrap and refrigerate for 1 hour, or as long as overnight.

**ASSEMBLE AND COOK**

**1.** Preheat your oven to 375°F.

**2.** Roll the dough 1/8 inch thick. Cut out rounds with

a 3 1/2-inch round cutter or the top of a glass, bowl, or any item you have handy that might work.

**3.** Cut out as many rounds as you can from the rolled-out dough. Place scraps back in the bowl, cover, and store in the refrigerator so the dough stays cool until you're ready to use it for the next round. You will want to handle the dough in turns like this to keep the butter from melting.

**4.** In a small bowl, make an egg wash by whisking together the egg and milk.

**5.** Hold each cut round of pastry in the palm of your hand and place 1 tablespoon of filling in the center.

**6.** Brush the egg wash along the edges of the round and then fold them together, wrapping the dough around the filling.

**7.** Crimp the edges with your fingers or a fork. I often use my fingers first and then go back and make them pretty with a fork.

**8.** Place the empanadas on a baking sheet and brush their tops with more egg wash.

**9.** If there is room for more empanadas on the baking sheet, store the prepared ones in the refrigerator while you make more empanadas to fill the tray. Continue to store the dough between rounds in the refrigerator to keep chilled.

**10.** Bake the empanadas in the oven for 20 minutes, or until golden brown.

**11.** Remove the empanadas from the oven and serve warm. If you have leftovers, you can keep them in the refrigerator for a few days or in the freezer for up to a month.

## APPLE CHICKEN EMPANADA FILLING

FILLS 20 TO 25 SMALL EMPANADAS

My daughter and I make these together. Cayenne, oregano, apples—these ingredients allow for the removal of obstacles to joy, with infinite reward. We make these every fall, after our annual trip to the orchard, and eat them for weeks on end. Batch after batch, evening after evening. Scooping, folding, and sealing, laughing, sharing, and devouring. It's an autumn on-repeat meal that never gets old.

¾ cup diced Granny Smith apple (diced into ¼-inch pieces; Gala apples work too)

Juice of ½ lemon or lime

1 tablespoon unsalted butter, cold and diced

1 cup diced red or white onion

2 garlic cloves, minced

1 ½ teaspoons chili powder

½ teaspoon dried oregano

½ teaspoon salt, or more to taste

Black pepper, to taste

2 cups diced cooked chicken

1 cup grated white cheddar cheese (the "off the block" or larger grate is best)

**1.** Toss the apple with the citrus juice and set aside.

**2.** Melt the butter in a skillet set over medium heat.

**3.** Add the onion and garlic to the skillet and cook while stirring for about 5 minutes, until the onion softens and the garlic smells unbearably delicious.

**4.** Add the chili powder, oregano, salt, and pepper. Then toss in the apple chunks and cook for about 2 minutes.

**5.** Mix in the chicken. Taste and adjust the seasoning if needed.

**6.** Remove the filling from the heat. Once cooled, stir in the cheddar.

**7.** This will keep for a few days in a tightly sealed container in the refrigerator, so making it ahead of time (along with the crust) can give you a fun family assembly activity on a weekend afternoon or a quick weekday meal.

## FAJITA BLACK BEAN EMPANADA FILLING

FILLS 20 TO 25 SMALL EMPANADAS

I am often on the lookout for fun meatless dinners, and these empanadas are perfect for them. Made ahead of time, they are ideal for a quick weekday dinner. Get some guacamole, chips, and salsa, maybe even some Spanish rice, and you have a feast on your hands! A delicious, wonderful feast. And with the black beans as the star, this is a great meal before a test or big decision for the clarity and truth they can provide.

1 tablespoon olive oil

1 cup chopped red onion

1 tablespoon minced garlic

15 ounces canned black beans, drained well

1 ½ cups chopped bell peppers (I use a mix of red and green)

1-ounce packet taco seasoning

1 ½ cups shredded sharp cheddar cheese, or a bag of premixed "Mexican cheese" from the store

**1.** Warm the oil in a skillet set over medium-high heat.

**2.** Add the onion and garlic and cook, stirring occasionally, until the garlic becomes fragrant and the onion becomes slightly transparent, 3 to 4 minutes.

**3.** Add the black beans, peppers, and taco seasoning and cook, stirring occasionally, for 5 to 7 minutes, until warmed through.

**4.** With a large spoon or potato masher, gently mash the black bean mixture. You don't need to make the mixture completely smooth; just mash it enough to give it a varied texture.

**5.** Stir in the cheese and steal a bite or two before you fill your crusts!

**6.** This will keep for a few days in a tightly sealed container in the refrigerator.

## POTATO CHORIZO EMPANADA FILLING

FILLS 20 TO 25 SMALL EMPANADAS

It's hard to think of a better way to take advantage of the grounding and stability that potatoes can provide than through the process of making and enjoying these empanadas. Not only that, but the spice in the sausage will remind you that while you want to stay grounded, you must also stay brave. Know who you are and find and hold on to your center while you reach ever outward and upward to be all that you aspire to be.

2 tablespoons olive oil

1 cup finely chopped chorizo

2 red onions, finely chopped

1 red bell pepper, finely chopped

½ cup finely chopped green bell pepper

3 garlic cloves, minced

1 ½ teaspoons sweet paprika

½ teaspoon cumin powder

½ teaspoon dried cilantro

¼ teaspoon crumbled dried oregano

¼ teaspoon salt

2 Yukon Gold or russet potatoes, peeled and diced small

¾ cup finely grated Manchego cheese

**1.** In a heavy saucepan, heat the oil over low to medium heat, then add the chorizo and cook, stirring occasionally, for about 5 minutes. Once cooked, transfer to a plate lined with paper towels to cool.

**2.** Add the onions to the same saucepan and cook over medium heat, stirring frequently, until golden and very soft, about 15 minutes.

**3.** Stir in the bell peppers, garlic, paprika, cumin, cilantro, oregano, and salt and cook, stirring frequently, until the peppers are soft, about 10 minutes.

**4.** Add the potatoes and cook, covered, for 10 to 12 minutes, until they are just barely tender. Stir every few minutes.

**5.** Stir the chorizo into the mixture until well combined, then transfer to a bowl.

**6.** Cool to room temperature and add the Manchego cheese. This mixture will keep in a tightly sealed container for up to 2 days, but I recommend using it once it's reached room temperature.

# Turkey Lentil Sloppy Joes

SERVES 6 TO 8

Sloppy joes always feel a bit celebratory to me. I have no good reason for this, but this meal always makes me happy. Perhaps because right in the name it eschews perfection and neatness. This is a meal meant to be, well, sloppy. We spend so much time trying to get things right, perfect, amazing. It's exhausting, honestly.

So put away the white shirts and tablecloths. Set aside notions of an impeccably plated meal, and embrace the mess. The mess of the sandwich, the kitchen, all the things. Embrace the idea that it's okay to be our purely imperfect selves living tremendously chaotic lives. Because in that there is undeniable beauty. And, even better, it comes with a side of Sweet Potato Fries.

1 green bell pepper, finely chopped

1 small onion, finely diced

1 tablespoon olive oil

1 pound ground turkey (optional)

1 cup water

1 cup chicken or vegetable broth

1 cup brown lentils, or 2 cups if omitting the turkey

3 garlic cloves, minced

1 cup tomato sauce

¼ cup ketchup

3 tablespoons tomato paste

*Ingredients continued on page 103*

**1.** In a large pot, cook the green pepper and onion in olive oil over medium heat until softened, about 4 minutes.

**2.** Add the turkey and cook, stirring occasionally, until browned.

**3.** Add the water, broth, lentils, and garlic and bring to a boil. Once boiling, reduce the heat to a simmer, cover, and allow to simmer for 25 minutes.

**4.** After 25 minutes, stir in all the remaining ingredients and simmer for an additional 10 to 15 minutes, or until thickened.

**5.** Spoon the lentil mixture over the hamburger buns and serve with desired toppings and a side of Sweet Potato Fries.

1 tablespoon apple cider
  vinegar
1 teaspoon Worcestershire
  sauce
1 teaspoon yellow mustard
2 tablespoons brown sugar
1 teaspoon chili powder

## FOR SERVING

6 to 8 hamburger buns,
  toasted
Shredded sharp cheddar
  cheese (optional)
Diced red onion (optional)
Sliced avocado (optional)
Yellow mustard (optional)
Chipotle Mayo (see page
  282; optional)
Sweet Potato Fries (see
  page 159)

financial security

lentil

# BBQ Shrimp SERVES 4

This can easily be made over a grill, with the sauce brushed on, or in a stovetop skillet. Either way, serve with a delicious corn and tomato salad and feel bright and summery any time of year.

2 teaspoons olive or
  avocado oil

1 pound raw large shrimp
  (26 to 30 shrimp per
  pound), peeled and
  deveined (I like to leave
  the tails on)

½ teaspoon salt, or more
  to taste

1 teaspoon black pepper, or
  more to taste

2 cups BBQ Sauce (see
  page 283), or more to taste

1 tablespoon chopped fresh
  parsley for garnishing

**FOR SERVING
(OPTIONAL)**

Corn Tomato Salad
  (see page 145)

Cheesy Grits (see page 158)

**1.** Heat the oil in a large skillet set over medium heat.

**2.** Add the shrimp in a single layer and sprinkle with salt and pepper.

**3.** Cook undisturbed for 2 to 3 minutes, then flip and cook for another minute or so, until the shrimp are pink and opaque.

**4.** Drizzle the BBQ Sauce over the cooked shrimp and toss the shrimp in the sauce to coat them.

**5.** Remove the shrimp from the heat; add more BBQ Sauce, salt, or pepper if desired; and divide among serving plates. Garnish each serving with parsley.

**6.** Serve alongside a Corn Tomato Salad or atop Cheesy Grits.

OPPOSITE: BBQ SHRIMP WITH CORN TOMATO SALAD (SEE PAGE 145)

# Lemon Garlic Shrimp SERVES 4

Lemon and garlic are not just a delicious combination but a powerful one. Garlic imbues protection, while lemons deter misfortune and revitalize. The combined effect makes this a wonderful meal to enjoy before heading out on a new adventure.

1 pound uncooked shrimp (26 to 30 shrimp per pound), peeled and deveined

1 teaspoon cumin powder

1 teaspoon crushed red pepper flakes, and more for garnishing

¾ teaspoon sea salt, or more to taste

¼ teaspoon black pepper, or more to taste

5 tablespoons and 1 teaspoon unsalted butter, divided

5 garlic cloves, thinly sliced

2 tablespoons lemon juice (freshly squeezed from ½ lemon), or more to taste

1 tablespoon dry white wine vinegar

*Ingredients continued on page 107*

**1.** Place the shrimp in a large mixing bowl.

**2.** In a separate small bowl, combine the cumin, red pepper flakes, sea salt, and black pepper, then pour the mixture into the bowl with the shrimp and toss the shrimp in the spices.

**3.** Melt 2 tablespoons butter in a large skillet set over medium-high heat. Add the garlic and cook until fragrant, about 1 minute.

**4.** Add the shrimp and cook, stirring frequently, until the shrimp starts to curl, 2 to 3 minutes.

**5.** Add the remaining 3 tablespoons and 1 teaspoon butter as well as the lemon juice and white wine vinegar.

**6.** Cook, stirring, until the butter melts and the shrimp have cooked through or the flesh is opaque and pink with no more gray, 4 to 5 minutes. Do not overcook; doing so is what

1 tablespoon chopped fresh
parsley for garnishing

Zest of 1 lemon for
garnishing

causes a rubbery texture.

**7.** Remove the shrimp from the heat and taste test, adding more lemon juice, salt, or pepper if desired.

**8.** Transfer the shrimp to a serving dish. Garnish with parsley, lemon zest, and red pepper flakes.

protection

garlic

# Pancetta Scallops SERVES 4

I used to be terrified to cook seafood. I grew up right in the middle of the country and had nothing in the realm of seafood aside from the occasional fried fish stick until well into college.

And given that fish was intimidating, scallops felt *way* too fancy for me to attempt. But I love scallops, and after they became my default order whenever they were available at a restaurant, I decided I needed to learn to make them at home. Imagine my surprise to find out that they are unbelievably easy to make.

This was not the only time I'd avoided something I would enjoy for fear it was too difficult to get right. I am loath to admit it, but this happens quite often. Things feel too fancy or any number of other descriptors I hesitate to align myself with, and I become convinced that I'm treading into territory where I don't belong and in which I will fail miserably.

But here's the thing: almost every time I actually try The Thing, I discover I'm wrong, that I'm capable. We are all capable of much more than we give ourselves credit for. So go make a meal that feels too much, too difficult, too fancy. Take the job, make the craft, speak at the place. Do all the things. You're amazing, and you deserve a yummy dinner of fancy scallops to honor that.

2 tablespoons olive oil

4 ounces pancetta, finely diced

16 ounces sea scallops

¼ teaspoon salt

½ teaspoon black pepper

**1.** Heat a skillet over medium heat.

**2.** Add the olive oil and pancetta and cook until crisp, about 3 minutes.

**3.** Remove the pancetta from the pan, leaving the oil and drippings, and set it aside.

**4.** Season the scallops with salt and pepper, being generous with the pepper.

**5.** Add the scallops to the pan and sear over medium-high heat for approximately 2 minutes on each side to brown. You will know that they are done properly when they feel like set Jell-O to the touch—firm with a soft give.

**6.** Remove the scallops from the pan, toss them with the pancetta, and serve.

# Aunt Judy's Étouffée SERVES 6 TO 8

This is my favorite recipe for Beltane, the early spring holiday that honors the uniting of the god and goddess. It is halfway between the spring equinox and the summer solstice and is about abundant love and true partnership. Beltane reminds us we are a "we" and that this fact is worth celebrating with every fiber of our being. This time of year is an opportunity for all of us to celebrate our present, where we are today and who we are with, as the gift it is. The life we have built is worth cherishing, and our greatest act should be to remain truly connected to all of it. On Beltane I like to remember the gift of that connection, the gift of the love of fairytales and living dreams. I know well I live a blessed life, and Beltane serves as a reminder for me to cherish that. And it's worth celebrating, not just one day in May but any day, every day.

My Aunt Judy had a recipe that serves just such a purpose. She lived a life with her great love, my Uncle Phil, and never was there a time when I couldn't palpably feel their connection when I was with them. Judy and Phil were reminders of a love that could last—of the possibility of two souls somehow weaving together a life and love that could stand the test of time. And so, I offer you her étouffée recipe: a little spicy, a lot delicious. Make it with love in your heart, and those you cherish will feel it and feel celebrated, I promise.

*Étouffée* is French and literally means "smothered." May you and the ones you love be absolutely smothered in everything wonderful on the glorious Beltane holiday and every day.

1 cup (2 sticks) unsalted butter

1 ½ cups chopped onions

1 ½ cups chopped celery or
  green bell peppers

¼ cup smoked paprika

1 tablespoon Tabasco
  sauce, or to taste

*Ingredients continued on*
  *page 111*

**1.** Place the butter in a large sauté pan set over medium heat. Add the onions and celery and cook, stirring occasionally, until the vegetables are soft.
**2.** Add the paprika and Tabasco. I find that how much Tabasco to add is totally a matter of taste. If you're nervous about how much to include, you can hold off until the end and add it over the cooked dish. For me it's a solid tablespoon, or 2 if I'm feeling sassy.
**3.** Add the flour and cornstarch in batches until

¼ cup and 1 tablespoon
all-purpose flour

2 tablespoons cornstarch

30 ounces chicken broth

2 pounds cooked and peeled
crawfish or shrimp (or a mix)

⅛ cup chopped green onion
tops (green parts only)

Creole Seasoning (see page
112) or store-bought Cajun
seasoning, to taste

6 cups cooked rice or
quinoa for serving
(optional)

## Tip
..........................

Aunt Judy's recipe calls for
the traditional celery, but
we substitute green bell
peppers in my house, as
Sam hates celery. Feel free
to do the same if someone
at your table has a similar
aversion. I like to toss my
shrimp lightly in some extra
seasoning and grill with
a touch of butter before
adding to the étouffée so
they're crisp, but cook them
however you find most tasty.

combined well, stirring constantly. The mixture will
be thick and clumpy.

**4.** Add the broth 1/2 cup at a time, then simmer for
20 minutes.

**5.** Add the crawfish or shrimp (or both!), green
onion tops, and Cajun seasoning. Simmer another
15 minutes.

**6.** Serve over cooked rice or quinoa. If you want to
get really fancy, pour each serving of étouffée into a
shallow bowl, then pack the rice or quinoa into a 1/4
cup or 1/2 cup measuring cup. Turn the cup carefully
over the center of the bowl, making a round of grains
in the middle of your étouffée.

# Creole Seasoning MAKES ABOUT 2/3 CUP

At my house we often use Tony Chachere's Creole Seasoning, and my cousin Kathy, Aunt Judy's oldest daughter, offered up a similar one by Walker & Sons called Slap Ya Mama, which I wish I had on hand simply for the name. If you can't find a premade Cajun or Creole seasoning in your local store, or you simply forgot to purchase one, this will work in a pinch.

3 tablespoons paprika (sweet is my recommendation)

2 tablespoons garlic powder

2 tablespoons onion powder

1 tablespoon dried thyme

1 tablespoon kosher salt or sea salt (optional)

1 tablespoon black pepper

2 teaspoons cayenne powder

**1.** Combine all ingredients.

## Tip

This seasoning is great for use on just about anything, so if I make it at home I will often double the recipe, as we tend to go through it pretty quickly. If your family isn't as seasoning-happy as mine, store it in a cool dark place and it should be good for 6 months.

# Springtime Asparagus Risotto SERVES 8

Springtime is a time of great anticipation. Winter can hang heavy and often lasts long. Our very souls can ache for the first touch of spring, that first warm day, that first glimpse of tulips in the store, crocuses peeking up between the ever-shrinking snowdrifts. Asparagus finally appearing on the shelves in great green bunches.

I always see this meal as a chance to pause and appreciate the turn of the season, to remember how lucky we were to have months where we could curl up indoors with each other and learn new things and plan new adventures, and how lucky we are to have months ahead of us to make them all real. The making of this meal, the slow turning of the spoon in the pot, the adding of the broth just a little at a time, reminds me to be patient. I take a breath and consider my hopes for the coming warm days. I appreciate, deeply, the moment in time I have to reflect and anticipate.

It is an anticipation of open days, long afternoons, road trips, and long, sunny walks—of all the days ahead filled with the bright yellows and greens just around the corner. And the pot is filled with them too, spinning and bubbling in front of me, fulfilling the promise of brighter, warmer days.

1 pound pancetta, diced

¼ cup olive oil, divided, and more for oiling the pan

2 bundles (approximately 2 pounds) asparagus

Salt, to taste

Black pepper, to taste

*Ingredients continued on page 115*

**1.** Fry the pancetta in a lightly oiled saucepan until crispy. Set aside on a paper towel.

**2.** Preheat your oven to 400°F.

**3.** Line up half the asparagus stalks and look at where the end of the stalks' green color starts to fade to white. Cut those ends off and dispose of them. Then cut the remaining stalks into 1-inch pieces.

**4.** Place the asparagus pieces on a baking sheet and toss in 2 tablespoons olive oil and generous amounts of salt and pepper. Roast for approximately 30 minutes, or until crisp.

4 cups low-sodium chicken
  broth, or more if needed in
  step 5

3 tablespoons unsalted butter

2 tablespoons olive oil

½ cup chopped yellow
  onion

3 garlic cloves, minced

1 ½ cups arborio rice

½ cup dry white wine

¼ cup grated Parmesan
  cheese, and more for
  serving

2 teaspoons turmeric
  powder

*Tip*
..........................

Eat at a table filled with
springtime tulips and
beautifully painted
eggs to celebrate the
gift of spring. Or enjoy
on any night filled with
flowers as a reminder
that warmer days,
literally or figuratively,
are always on their way.

**5.** Reserve the tops of the asparagus for garnish.
Place the rest of the asparagus into a food processor
and process until smooth. Add water or chicken
broth if necessary to create a purée, but try to avoid
using more than 2 tablespoons, as you don't want it
to be runny.

**6.** Melt the butter in a pot set over medium heat.
Add the remaining 2 tablespoons olive oil.

**7.** Stir in the onion and garlic and cook, stirring
occasionally, until soft and fragrant.

**8.** Add the arborio rice, stirring it into the butter,
onion, and garlic. Make sure to toast every piece of
rice to golden but not dark brown. This will take 3 to
5 minutes.

**9.** Slowly pour in the white wine. Then add the
chicken broth 1/4 cup at a time, stirring each
batch of liquid until it's absorbed before adding the
next 1/4 cup.

**10.** Once all the broth has been poured into the
pot and mostly absorbed into the rice, stir in the
asparagus purée and Parmesan.

**11.** Add the turmeric. This will impart a warm flavor
as well as a lovely yellow color.

**12.** Season with salt and pepper to taste.

**13.** Top each serving with your reserved roasted
asparagus tops, pancetta, and Parmesan.

# Summer Corn Risotto SERVES 8

Abundance and love. Prosperity and passion. A meal to bring all good things to yourself and those you love. Bright, colorful, and creamy, this Summer Corn Risotto can't help but bring a smile to your face and a feeling of summer to your soul.

5 ears corn

4 cups low-sodium chicken
  or vegetable broth

3 tablespoons unsalted
  butter

3 tablespoons olive oil

½ cup diced yellow onion

4 garlic cloves, minced

1 cup arborio rice

¼ cup pecorino cheese

Salt, to taste

Black pepper, to taste

Ingredients continued on

  page 117

**1.** Cut the corn off the cobs, reserving 3 empty cobs to make a broth. Set the corn aside.

**2.** Combine the broth and 3 empty cobs in a large pot and bring to a simmer over low heat. Let simmer for 20 to 30 minutes.

**3.** Remove the broth from the heat, let cool, and remove the cobs. Set the broth aside.

**4.** Melt the butter in a pot set over medium heat. Add the olive oil.

**5.** Stir in the onion and garlic and cook, stirring occasionally, until soft and fragrant, about 2 minutes.

**6.** Add the arborio rice, stirring it into the butter, onion, and garlic. Make sure to toast every piece of rice to golden but not dark brown. This will take 3 to 5 minutes.

**7.** Slowly add the corn broth 1/4 cup at a time, stirring until it is absorbed before adding the next 1/4 cup. *A lot of people shy away from risotto because of this step with its stirring and waiting. It can feel monotonous, but it's a process I've come to savor. This is the perfect time to ground yourself; feel the floor beneath your feet, relax your shoulders, breathe in during one turn of the spoon, and breathe out the next. Let the process lead you, and let go of*

## FOR SERVING

Chopped chives

1 pint cherry tomatoes,
   quartered

Shredded pecorino cheese

Black pepper, to taste

*all your other worries and chores and things to be done. Let your spoon match your breath, and allow yourself the time to just be.*

**8.** Once all the broth has been added and is mostly absorbed into the arborio rice, stir in the pecorino.

**9.** Season with salt and pepper to taste.

**10.** Top each serving with chives, cherry tomato pieces, more cheese, and black pepper.

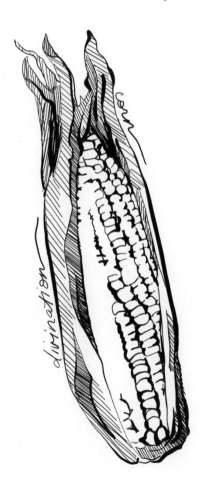

# Creamy Garlic Risotto SERVES 8

Slow to come together, an exercise in patience and fortitude, this Creamy Garlic Risotto brings garlic to the forefront and emphasizes the intention of protection. Take the time to focus on each step, carefully watching as the ingredients coalesce to form your dish, all the while absorbing not just broth and wine but a hope for safety to be delivered securely from one point to the other. This is a meal, but it is more than that; it is a refuge and a sanctuary, an opportunity to share in comfort and assurance.

4 tablespoons unsalted butter

2 tablespoons olive oil

1 cup diced white onion

7 garlic cloves, minced

1 cup arborio rice

½ cup white wine

3 cups chicken or vegetable broth

¾ cup grated Parmesan cheese

Salt, to taste

Black pepper, to taste

**FOR SERVING**

Chopped fresh parsley

Shredded Parmesan cheese

**1.** Melt the butter in a pot set over medium heat, then add the olive oil.

**2.** Stir in the onion and garlic and cook, stirring occasionally, until soft and fragrant, 3 to 4 minutes.

**3.** Add the arborio rice, stirring it into the butter, onion, and garlic. Make sure to toast every piece to golden but not dark brown. This will take 3 to 5 minutes.

**4.** Pour in the white wine and stir until absorbed.

**5.** Slowly add the broth 1/4 cup at a time, stirring until it is mostly absorbed before adding the next 1/4 cup.

**6.** Once all the broth has been added and mostly absorbed into the arborio rice, stir in the Parmesan.

**7.** Season with salt and pepper to taste.

**8.** Top each serving with parsley and Parmesan.

# Butternut Squash Risotto SERVES 8

Filled with the flavors of late autumn, tripping over into the long nights of winter, the ingredients in this dish invite us to look inward, to summon the courage to trust ourselves and love ourselves as we move forward on our path. Challenges once seemingly unsolvable can feel approachable in this renewed confidence.

16 ounces butternut squash, diced into 1-inch pieces

5 tablespoons olive oil, divided

1 cup broccolini, stems cut off and cut into bite-size pieces

1 teaspoon nutmeg powder

1 teaspoon red pepper flakes

4 tablespoons unsalted butter

1 cup diced white onion

7 garlic cloves, minced

1 cup arborio rice

½ cup white wine

3 cups chicken or vegetable broth

1 cup grated Parmesan cheese

*Ingredients continued on page 121*

**1.** Preheat your oven to 400°F.

**2.** Place the squash in a roasting pan, toss in 2 tablespoons olive oil, and roast for 20 minutes.

**3.** Push the squash to the side and add the broccolini to the pan. Toss in 1 tablespoon olive oil and roast for another 20 minutes.

**4.** Remove the pan from the oven and set the broccolini and half the squash aside.

**5.** Place the remaining half of the squash, the nutmeg, and the red pepper flakes in a food processor or blender and purée until smooth, or to your desired consistency.

**6.** Melt the butter in a saucepan set over medium heat, then add the remaining 2 tablespoons olive oil.

**7.** Stir in the onion and garlic and cook, stirring occasionally, until soft and fragrant, 3 to 4 minutes.

**8.** Add the arborio rice, stirring it into the butter, onion, and garlic. Make sure to toast every piece to golden but not dark brown. This will take 3 to 5 minutes.

**9.** Pour in the white wine and stir until absorbed.

**10.** Slowly add the broth 1/4 cup at a time, stirring until it is mostly absorbed before adding the next 1/4 cup.

Salt, to taste

Black pepper, to taste

**FOR SERVING**

Finely diced pancetta,
 cooked until crispy

Fresh parsley

Shredded Parmesan cheese

**11.** Once all the broth has been added to the pot, stir in the Parmesan.

**12.** Fold in the butternut squash purée.

**13.** Season with salt and pepper to taste.

**14.** Top with the roasted squash and broccolini, pancetta, parsley, and more Parmesan.

# Spicy Turkey Enchiladas SERVES 8

These spicy enchiladas were the first meal Sam and I ever made together. They were initially made in a microscopic kitchen in my Kips Bay studio apartment, and almost twenty years later we are still making meals and magic together. Will these enchiladas always spark true love? I can't make any promises, but find someone you adore to make them with, and it might just be the first of a lifetime of delicious moments.

## FILLING

2 tablespoons extra virgin olive oil

1 pound ground turkey (you can also use beef)

1 red onion, diced

½ large white onion, diced

1 cup shredded cheddar cheese

½ cup sour cream

2 tablespoons chopped fresh parsley

¼ teaspoon black pepper

## SAUCE

15 ounces tomato sauce

⅓ cup water

⅓ cup chopped green bell pepper

Ingredients continued on page 124

**1.** Grease a 10-inch skillet with the olive oil and then set it over medium heat and cook the turkey, stirring occasionally, until it browns, approximately 10 minutes. Once the turkey is browned, drain the excess oil and return the skillet to the stove with the heat off.

**2.** Stir the red and white onions, cheddar, sour cream, parsley, and black pepper into the turkey. Cover to keep warm.

**3.** Preheat your oven to 350°F.

**4.** To make the sauce, in a pot set over high heat, mix together the tomato sauce, water, bell pepper, green chilis, jalapeños, garlic, chili powders, oregano, and cumin, and bring to a boil.

**5.** Reduce the heat to low and let simmer, uncovered, for 5 minutes, stirring occasionally.

**6.** Pour the sauce into a round cake pan, pie plate, or any round shallow container. Let sit a few minutes to cool slightly.

¼ cup or one 4-ounce
  can chopped green chili
  peppers

2 jalapeños, chopped

2 garlic cloves, minced

2 teaspoons chili powder

2 teaspoons chipotle chili
  powder

1 teaspoon dried oregano

½ teaspoon cumin powder

## FOR SERVING

8 medium tortillas (corn or
  flour)

Shredded cheddar cheese

Sour cream

Chives

Chopped red onions

Chopped jalapeños

## ASSEMBLE AND COOK

**1.** Dip each tortilla into your shallow bowl of sauce, taking care to coat both sides, and then place onto an ungreased 7-by-11-by-1 1/2-inch or similar-size baking dish.

**2.** Scoop 1/4 cup of the turkey mixture onto each tortilla and roll. Continue until you fill the dish with rolled tortillas.

**3.** Pour the remaining sauce over the enchiladas and top with additional cheese to taste.

**4.** Bake uncovered in the oven for 20 minutes, until the enchiladas are bubbling and any added cheese is nicely melted.

**5.** Garnish with sour cream, chives, red onion, and jalapeño.

desire

bell pepper

# Cauliflower Poblano Enchiladas SERVES 6

In all honesty, it took me a while to develop this recipe. I had a hard time believing I could create meat-free enchiladas not overwhelmingly stuffed with cheese that would still be tasty and satisfying. However, not for the first time (nor, inevitably, the last), I was dead wrong. These have quickly become a favorite at my table. They're perfect to make during a full moon, as cauliflower is associated with the symbology of the moon and a denotation of our own many phases and multitudes. The cauliflower is paired here with the energy of the poblano, a banisher of negative energy and multiplier of courage. You can't help but feel good consuming this meal.

## FILLING

2 medium cauliflower heads

1 teaspoon cumin powder

1 teaspoon coriander powder

1 teaspoon smoked paprika

1 teaspoon chipotle chili powder

½ teaspoon cayenne powder

½ teaspoon salt

1 teaspoon black pepper

3 tablespoons olive oil, or more if needed to cover cauliflower

1 ½ cups shredded white cheddar cheese

*Ingredients continued on page 127*

**1.** Preheat your oven to 425°F.

**2.** Remove the stems from your cauliflower and clean off all green leaves.

**3.** Chop the cauliflower into small, bite-size pieces. Be sure to scoop up and include the "crumbs" that result as well. This should yield about 3 cups of cauliflower pieces.

**4.** In a small bowl, combine the cumin, coriander, paprika, chipotle chili powder, cayenne, salt, and pepper.

**5.** Spread the chopped cauliflower across a large baking sheet.

**6.** Drizzle olive oil over the cauliflower and sprinkle the spice mix on top. Cover as much of the cauliflower as possible with both.

**7.** Toss the cauliflower with your hands, again distributing as much of the spice and oil as possible. If it feels dry, add more oil, 1 teaspoon at a time. You

1 shallot or ½ onion, finely
  diced

## SAUCE

1 poblano chili pepper

2 tablespoons unsalted
  butter

1 shallot, finely diced

2 ½ tablespoons
  all-purpose flour

1 ¼ cups chicken or
  vegetable broth or stock

½ cup sour cream

1 teaspoon coriander
  powder

Salt, to taste

Pepper, to taste

## FOR SERVING

6 medium tortillas (corn or
  flour)

Shredded cheddar cheese
  (optional)

Fresh cilantro

Chopped green onions

don't want it to be wet, just damp enough to hold the spice and brown while baking.

**8.** Roast the cauliflower until it's tender to the touch and the edges start to get crispy, 25 to 30 minutes.

**9.** While your cauliflower is roasting, cook the poblano chili pepper for your sauce until blackened and blistered. To do so, either place the poblano directly over the flame of a gas stovetop and turn frequently, cooking 3 to 5 minutes on each side; place it in your oven using the broil setting for 10 to 15 minutes, turning often; or place it in the oven using your oven's hottest temperature setting. If you don't have a gas stovetop or an oven with a broil setting, it may take a bit longer to blister, but I promise it works!

**10.** Once your pepper is ready, remove it from the heat and place it in a bowl with a towel covering it to allow it to continue to steam. Let it rest 10 to 15 minutes.

**11.** Once cool, use your fingers to rub the blistered skin off the pepper and seed it.

**12.** When the cauliflower has finished roasting, place it in a large bowl and add the white cheddar and diced shallot or onion. Stir well and set aside. Leave the oven on.

**13.** To make the sauce, finely chop the roasted poblano chili pepper. I recommend taste testing a small amount of your pepper to decide how much to use. Poblano chilis are normally spicy but mild; however, every once in a while you get a hot one. If

you take a small taste now you can decide if you want to use the whole pepper in your sauce or just half.

**14.** Heat a saucepan over medium-high heat and melt your butter in it. Add the shallot and stir for about 3 minutes, until the shallot begins to soften.

**15.** Whisk in the flour. This will begin to make a roux, which will help thicken your sauce.

**16.** Continue to whisk, keeping the sauce smooth, as you add the broth in small amounts.

**17.** Remove the sauce from the heat and add the finely chopped poblano, sour cream, coriander, salt, and pepper while continuing to whisk until smooth and combined.

**ASSEMBLE AND COOK**

**1.** Lightly grease a 7-by-11-by-1 1/2-inch or similar-size baking dish and pour 1/3 cup poblano sauce into the bottom of the pan.

**2.** Wrap 1/3 cup cauliflower filling into each tortilla and place each seam side down in the pan.

**3.** Once all the enchiladas are filled and in the pan, pour the remaining sauce over them.

**4.** Cover with foil and bake for 20 minutes, then remove the foil and bake another 15 minutes, adding some cheddar to the top if you'd like.

**5.** Top with cilantro and green onions, and dig in!

# Creamy Chicken Enchiladas SERVES 6

Ah, the potential of a blank page, a white canvas . . . an open mind. When you are searching for a way to clear your mind and make space to begin something anew, this is the perfect meal. (It's also perfect any time you feel like something creamy and cheesy!) The sweetness of the corn adds the promise of prosperity in your current ventures and whatever may come after.

## FILLING

2 pounds Chicken Carnitas
(see page 82), shredded

1 cup Salsa Verde (see page 279)

½ cup shredded mozzarella cheese

1 cup shredded white cheddar cheese

½ cup sweet corn

1 jalapeño, chopped

## SAUCE

2 tablespoons unsalted butter

2 tablespoons all-purpose flour

*Ingredients continued on page 130*

**1.** Stir together the chicken, Salsa Verde, cheeses, corn, and jalapeño until well combined, then set aside.

**2.** In a medium saucepan, melt the butter and whisk in the flour to make a roux. Once well combined, add the broth and continue to whisk until smooth. Simmer over low heat for 5 to 7 minutes, until the sauce is thick and bubbly.

**3.** Remove the pan from the heat and add the sour cream and green chilis.

**4.** Season with salt and pepper.

## ASSEMBLE AND COOK

**1.** Preheat your oven to 350°F. Lightly grease a 7-by-11-by-1 1/2-inch or similar-size baking dish with the oil.

**2.** Scoop 1/4 to 1/2 cup of chicken mixture into each tortilla, roll closed, and place in the baking dish.

**3.** Once all the enchiladas are filled and in the pan, pour the sauce over them.

1 ½ cups low-sodium or
  no-sodium-added
  chicken broth

½ cup sour cream

¼ cup or one 4-ounce
  can chopped green chili
  peppers

Salt, to taste

Black pepper, to taste

**FOR SERVING**

6 medium flour tortillas

Shredded mozzarella
  cheese

Shredded white cheddar
  cheese

Chopped fresh parsley

Salsa Verde (see page 279)

**4.** Bake for 25 minutes, or until the top starts to brown.

**5.** Top with additional cheese, parsley, and Salsa Verde, and serve.

# Black Bean Burgers SERVES 6

The symbology associated with the ingredients of this dish reflects almost too much goodness to be possible: clarity, love, desire, the uncovering of possibility, *and* the banishment of negative energy. May every time you make these be filled with such promise and the potential of such connection.

30 ounces canned black
beans (two 15-ounce
cans), drained

1 cup rolled oats (or bread
crumbs, in a pinch)

1 red onion, diced small

1 green bell pepper, diced
small

7 ounces canned chipotle
pepper in adobo sauce,
drained and roughly diced

4 garlic cloves, minced

1 teaspoon cumin powder

½ teaspoon garlic
powder

½ teaspoon smoked
paprika

2 tablespoons ketchup

*Ingredients continued on
page 134*

**1.** Preheat the oven to 325°F.

**2.** Spread the beans out on a baking sheet lined with parchment paper. Place in the oven for about 15 minutes to dry out.

**3.** In a medium bowl, mix together the oats, onion, green pepper, chipotle pepper, garlic, cumin, garlic powder, paprika, ketchup, and Worcestershire sauce.

**4.** Once thoroughly mixed, add the beans, feta, and eggs. I find using my hands helps to mix everything well and allows for smashing some of the beans to vary the texture a bit.

**5.** Use 1/3 cup of the mixture to make each patty, laying them onto a baking sheet or large plate. Chill the patties in the refrigerator for 15 minutes.

**6.** After the patties are chilled, place them in a lightly oiled skillet set over medium-low heat.

**7.** Cook each patty for 4 minutes per side, making sure to get a good char and sear.

OPPOSITE: BLACK BEAN BURGERS WITH SWEET POTATO FRIES (SEE PAGE 159)
AND CHIPOTLE MAYO (SEE PAGE 282).

1 tablespoon
  Worcestershire sauce
1 cup 1-inch pieces feta
  cheese
2 eggs
Extra virgin olive oil for
  cooking

**FOR SERVING**

6 slices sharp cheddar
  cheese (optional)
6 hamburger buns, toasted
Sliced avocado (optional)
Other toppings of choice
  (optional)

**8.** If topping with cheese, in the last minute, place a slice of cheese on each burger and partially cover (vent a lid, or use a large plate) so the cheese gets melty.

**9.** Place each patty on a toasted bun and top with avocado or your other favorite toppings!

*Only Small Actors*

# SALADS, SNACKS, AND SIDES

**A LITTLE OF THIS,** a little of that, bits and pieces, additions and enhancements—salads, snacks, and sides are accoutrements to a meal that somehow make it feel full and finished, that can take it from a quick bite to a multicourse meal. Sometimes a snack or side is a meal unto itself, and sometimes it is merely a way to tide one over on a busy afternoon. Always, it is a reminder that a supporting role can make all the difference.

# Cheesy Corn Casserole SERVES 8

This is a simple dish that feels special. A tradition at our Thanksgivings we get to spend at home, it can feel almost soufflé-like in texture without all the fuss. Make a little more of the hot sauce and sour cream mixture to put on top to serve, if you'd like.

Nonstick cooking spray

1 cup sliced onion

3 tablespoons unsalted
   butter

8 ½ ounces boxed corn
   bread mix or corn muffin
   mix

1 cup creamed corn

½ cup milk

1 cup sour cream

1 dash hot pepper sauce

1 cup shredded sharp
   cheddar cheese

**1.** Preheat your oven to 350°F.

**2.** Spray a 10-by-10-inch pan with nonstick cooking spray.

**3.** Heat a nonstick or cast-iron skillet over medium heat. Add the onion and butter to the pan and sauté for 3 to 5 minutes, until soft. Set aside.

**4.** In a separate bowl, combine the corn bread mix, corn, and milk.

**5.** In another bowl, mix the sour cream and hot sauce until well combined.

**6.** Pour the corn mixture into the baking dish and top with a layer of the onion slices, followed by the sour cream mixture and then the cheddar.

**7.** Bake uncovered for 15 minutes, then cover and bake for an additional 15 minutes.

# Macaroni and Cheese SERVES 8

Who doesn't love a bowl of macaroni and cheese from time to time? Not only is it a satis-fying side dish, it is a wonderful throwback to afternoons spent coloring, toppling blocks, and enjoying after-school specials. Boxed mac and cheese with its tiny noodles and orange powder is often the first meal we learn to cook all on our own and one a lot of us carry far into our futures. I know I always have a box of some kind stored in our pantry, just in case. In case of *what*, I'm not sure. But it's there, and I'm the better for it.

This recipe admittedly takes longer than the boxed version, but it's for sure worth the extra 20 minutes it may cost you for the comfort and sense of home it can evoke. Paprika itself is transformative, and in this dish, somewhere between the scent of smokiness and the threads of cheese trailing from your fork, a simpler time can be magically invoked. While I encourage you to make this your new default version, just know that if you end up pulling out that box some nights, I won't judge you.

16 ounces elbow macaroni

6 tablespoons unsalted
  butter, divided

¼ cup and 2 tablespoons
  all-purpose flour

1 teaspoon mustard powder

1 teaspoon black pepper

1 teaspoon seasoned salt,
  or more to taste

1 teaspoon smoked paprika

3 cups 2 percent milk

*Ingredients continued on
  page 140*

**1.** Preheat your oven to 350°F.

**2.** Cook the macaroni by following its package's instructions and cooking until it's al dente (still a bit firm), then drain and transfer to a 9-by-13-inch casserole dish.

**3.** Melt 4 tablespoons of the butter in a medium skillet set over low heat. Gradually add the flour, whisking until well combined.

**4.** Add the mustard powder, black pepper, seasoned salt, and paprika and continue to whisk.

**5.** Slowly pour in the milk 1/2 cup at a time, whisking constantly until smooth.

**6.** Stir in the cheeses.

2 cups shredded sharp
  cheddar cheese

1 cup shredded Colby-Jack
  cheese

1 cup grated Parmesan
  cheese

½ cup bread crumbs

**FOR SERVING**

Bacon crumbles

Roasted veggies (such as
  broccoli florets), chopped

Crispy Chicken (see page
  65)

**7.** Cook over low heat until the cheeses are melted and the sauce is thickened. A wooden spoon should leave a trail in the sauce after about 5 minutes.

**8.** Pour the sauce over the macaroni and stir well.

**9.** Melt the remaining 2 tablespoons of butter in a skillet set over medium heat. Add the bread crumbs and cook until browned.

**10.** Spread the bread crumbs over the macaroni and cheese, covering the noodles.

**11.** Bake for 30 minutes.

**12.** If you'd like to make this into a super hearty meal, top with crumbled bacon, roasted vegetables, Crispy Chicken, or any combination thereof!

# Pear Arugula Salad SERVES 2

We had a salad similar to this on a trip to the Cinque Terre on Italy's west coast. We found ourselves unexpectedly on an ages-old stone patio overlooking the ocean just as the sun was slipping behind the horizon. The air smelled of salt and honey, and the faces of the three people I love most were bathed in the most beautiful pink light, perfectly reflective of the sheer contentment and delight written across their faces. It felt like a moment too good to be true, and I make this salad to remind myself that moments like that happen—maybe more often than we realize.

This easy salad is prepared in minutes, and after making it I like to slow down, treasure each bite, and remember the feeling of sun and sand, wind and stone. I also remember to look around, to take in where I am at the moment, and to treasure that too.

5 ounces arugula

3 pears, thinly sliced

3 ounces shaved pecorino cheese or crumbled goat cheese

1 ounce roasted walnuts

Honey for drizzling (for a kick try the Serrano Hot Honey on page 268)

**1.** Spread the arugula across a large platter or plate.

**2.** Layer on pear slices and cheese.

**3.** Sprinkle walnuts on top and drizzle with honey.

# Kale Apple Salad SERVES 4

I made this salad one late summer evening in an attempt to find something that had at least one ingredient everyone liked. It was one of those days. Admittedly, there is always a lot of careful picking out of elements from the bowl and silently setting them aside being done by my children, particularly my son. Still, it's one of our favorite concoctions. The ingredients symbolize rebirth, rejuvenation, and longevity, and while the salad might be picked apart by tiny fingers, my intention to impart that we forever have the opportunity to start something new, to begin again so we may revive our hearts, remains intact.

¼ cup and 2 tablespoons
   lemon juice

¼ cup olive oil

Sea salt, to taste

10 ounces or 1 bunch kale
   leaves, chopped

2 apples (preferably
   Honeycrisp or Fuji), cored
   and sliced into matchsticks

¾ cup shredded pecorino
   cheese

⅓ cup chopped dates (dried
   cranberries also work and
   require no chopping!)

¼ cup slivered almonds

**1.** Create your lemon dressing by combining the lemon juice, olive oil, and a pinch of sea salt in a jar and shaking vigorously. You can also place the ingredients in a small food processor or blender and blend to make sure they are fully combined. Taste and season as desired.

**2.** Toss the kale with about one-third of the dressing, then set the dressed kale in the refrigerator to chill for 15 to 20 minutes.

**3.** Once the kale has chilled, remove it from the fridge and toss with the apple slices, pecorino, dates (or cranberries), and almonds, adding additional dressing to taste.

# Broccoli Salad SERVES 6

This is a staple of every picnic and warm-weather potluck I have ever been to, and for good reason: it is delicious, and only gets better if it sits a bit before you eat it. The perfect make-ahead dish, it offers a small reminder that it's okay to sit and take a rest before rushing off to your next chore or activity. We may just be better for the time out.

1 pound broccoli florets,
  chopped
¾ cup shredded sharp
  cheddar cheese
½ cup chopped pecans
⅛ cup dried cranberries
¼ cup chopped red onions
4 slices bacon, cooked and
  roughly chopped
1 cup mayonnaise
½ cup sugar
¼ cup apple cider vinegar
Salt, to taste
Black pepper, to taste

**1.** Combine broccoli, cheddar, pecans, dried cranberries, green onions, and bacon in a large bowl.

**2.** In a small bowl, whisk together the mayo, sugar, and apple cider vinegar until smooth and well combined. Add salt and pepper to taste.

**3.** Pour the mayo dressing over the broccoli mixture and stir well to combine.

**4.** Ideally refrigerate for 1 hour before serving, though I'm not going to stop you from digging in right away—I mean, it's *broccoli*! You're eating your greens!

# Corn Tomato Salad SERVES 4

A wonderful dish for summer or when you simply long for lazy afternoons, this salad works well with either freshly harvested corn and tomatoes from your garden or frozen bags and store-bought pints of produce. Whether reveling in these veggies when they're in-season or longing for them at a different time of year, this salad will usher in the perfect taste of an endless summer afternoon.

Salt, for the cooking water

4 ears fresh corn or 16 ounces frozen corn

¼ cup olive oil

1 tablespoon red wine vinegar

1 pint cherry tomatoes, halved

1 cup crumbled feta cheese

2 tablespoons dried marjoram

**1.** Bring a large pot of salted water to a boil. Add the corn and boil until tender, about 5 minutes.

**2.** Whisk the oil and red wine vinegar in a medium bowl, and then add the corn, tomatoes, feta, and marjoram. Gently stir to make sure everything is coated.

protection from discord

marjoram

# Dill Potato Salad SERVES 8

There are a million versions of potato salad. This one contains copious amounts of dill, a protection from evil, accompanied by, obviously, potatoes, which provide their own form of protection via grounding and stability. A true portent of protection, all from a meager, common salad? Not too shabby. And delicious, to boot.

7 red, fingerling, or Yukon new potatoes, diced

Salt, for the cooking water

6 eggs

8 radishes, grated

4 green onions, sliced

3 tablespoons chopped fresh dill weed

¾ cup mayonnaise

1 teaspoon spicy mustard or Dijon mustard

½ teaspoon sea salt

¼ teaspoon black pepper

**1.** Place the potatoes in a large pot and fill the pot with water, making sure the water is at least 1 inch above the tops of the potatoes.

**2.** Generously salt the water and bring to a boil.

**3.** Reduce to a simmer and cook for 20 minutes, or until the potatoes are tender and a fork inserts easily with only a little resistance.

**4.** Once the potatoes have finished cooking, rinse them with cold water and set them aside.

**5.** Add a few inches of cold water to a medium pot. Place the eggs in a single layer at the bottom of the pot, adding more water if necessary so that the eggs are covered by at least 1 to 2 inches of water.

**6.** Place the eggs over high heat, uncovered, and bring the water to a rolling boil.

**7.** Once the water is at a healthy boil, cover the pot and turn off the heat. Let the pot sit for 12 to 15 minutes.

**8.** Strain the hot water from the pan or carefully remove the eggs and place into a strainer. Run cold water over the eggs until they are cool to the touch.

**9.** Peel and then quarter the eggs and set them aside.

**10.** Let the eggs and potatoes cool completely, then place them in the refrigerator for 10 to 15 minutes.

**11.** In a large bowl, combine the radishes, green onions, dill, mayonnaise, mustard, sea salt, and pepper. Stir well to completely combine.

**12.** Once your potatoes and eggs are fully cooled, add them to your mayonnaise mixture. Stir gently until well combined.

*grounding*

*potato*

*dill soother*

# Artichoke Parmesan Stuffing SERVES 10

I made this stuffing for the first Thanksgiving that Sam and I shared. I wanted to make something special and was determined not to make stuffing from a box (which I was raised on, so this sudden departure remains unexplained). I scoured recipes, and while the initial version was a hit, I spent the years after slowly adjusting and improving until Sam told me to stop messing with it; he liked it as it was, and he was afraid I'd never get back to this particular variant. I let it be, and now this version is our official holiday stuffing.

Every year, this is the recipe I use, and it feels right to have artichoke, a symbol of patience and joy, be a main ingredient in this dish. As I now look back at all the years it took to get here, the experiments and trials, the holidays and dinners, I have to smile. It's been a good journey, and it is one that is far from over. There are so many meals we have yet to share and be thankful for.

6 to 8 cups 1-inch cubes
   crustless sourdough bread
   or similar bread
3 tablespoons olive oil
3 Italian sweet sausages,
   casings removed
3 Italian hot sausages,
   casing removed
2 cups chopped yellow
   onions
6 garlic cloves, minced
8 ounces frozen artichoke
   hearts, thawed and
   coarsely chopped

*Ingredients continued on*
   *page 151*

**1.** Preheat your oven to 350°F.

**2.** Spread the bread cubes out in a single layer across a couple of baking sheets and bake for 15 minutes, or until the cubes are toasted and dry, but not hard. They will feel a bit like day-old bread, but not croutons. There may be places they still feel squishy, and that's OK—the squishy parts soak up flavor while the crusty parts add texture.

**3.** Remove the bread cubes from the oven and set them aside. Keep the oven on.

**4.** Heat the oil in a large skillet set over medium-high heat. Add the sausages and cook for about 5 minutes, breaking up the sausages into bite-size pieces with a wooden spoon or spatula as they cook.

**5.** Add the onions and garlic and cook, stirring occasionally, until the onions are soft, the garlic

2 teaspoons chopped
  fresh thyme

1 ½ cups (5 to 6 ounces)
  freshly grated
  Parmesan cheese

1 cup low-sodium chicken
  broth, or more if needed

Salt, to taste

Black pepper, to taste

1 teaspoon unsalted butter,
  and more for greasing
  the foil

is fragrant, and the sausage has cooked through, another 5 to 7 minutes.

**6.** Mix in the artichoke hearts and thyme and sauté for another few minutes.

**7.** Transfer the mixture to a large bowl, then add the bread cubes and Parmesan. Toss well.

**8.** Set aside 1/4 cup broth to use in step 11. Pour the remaining broth over the bread mixture and stir until everything is moistened but not soaking. If you find dry spots, add more broth a bit at a time in the necessary places.

**9.** Season with salt and pepper to taste.

**10.** Use 1 teaspoon butter to grease a 9-by-13-inch baking dish, coating it well. Generous buttering is what makes those crispy edges that are so delicious.

**11.** Add the stuffing to the pan and drizzle the reserved 1/4 cup broth over the stuffing.

**12.** Take a large piece of aluminum foil and run a stick of butter along the underside of it. Place it over the stuffing dish and seal well.

**13.** Bake for 40 minutes, then remove the foil.

**14.** Bake for another 20 minutes, or until the top is crisp and golden.

# Cranberry Sauce SERVES 6

For our first Thanksgiving in New York City, our friend Tim rode the bus from Virginia to join us. I was thrilled to fix us a full holiday dinner with all the trimmings despite our minuscule hundred-year-old kitchen. As I was planning our menu, I asked Tim what special dish I could add to our dinner that would bring him a bit of home. He requested cranberry sauce in the can, specifically served so you could still see the ridges in the can-shaped cranberry blob.

Full disclosure: I was a tad disappointed. I was ready to do something amazingly fancy for him! But you know what? His request saved me. I was so busy cooking the rest of the meal, that side gave me a minute to breathe, and a smile to boot. Telling the story of how Tim added canned cranberries to our menu became a regular Thanksgiving tradition.

Almost two decades later, we found ourselves on Cape Cod for Thanksgiving, and I wandered the aisles of a tremendously large grocery store, collecting all of our needed ingredients. I passed a giant barrel filled to the brim with fresh cranberries and knew exactly what I'd be making for one of our sides. I admit later as I glanced down at our fully set table I had a moment of pause and longing, less for a can-shaped blob and more for the presence of a dear friend cracking jokes and passing plates. I look forward to when we can share the holiday again, with so many extra chairs at the table now we could easily serve both versions of this side over even louder laughter. Until then, we will continue to tell the story of Tim's one Thanksgiving request.

Cranberries stir up and support open communication—so in whatever form you may find them on your table, the stories and laughter are bound to flow.

½ cup orange juice

Zest of 1 medium orange

¼ cup sugar

8 ounces fresh or frozen
  cranberries

Pinch cinnamon powder
  (optional)

**1.** Combine the orange juice and zest in a medium saucepan set over high heat and bring to a boil.

**2.** Stir in the sugar and allow it to dissolve.

**3.** Add the cranberries and bring the mixture back to a boil.

**4.** Turn the heat to low and simmer for 10 minutes, until about half of the cranberries burst.

**5.** Add the cinnamon.

**6.** Remove the sauce from the heat and mash it with the back of a wooden spoon until your perfect consistency is reached.

# Cheddar Mashed Potatoes SERVES 6

These mashed potatoes are cheesy and creamy and all the good things, with a subtle hint of that special *something*, the hint of an ingredient that makes all the difference. The nutmeg in this dish is supposed to provide insight to those who use and ingest it, but for me in this particular recipe, the insight it brings is that even the smallest of unexpected gestures can make a difference. We often find ourselves at a juncture, a place where we don't know how to react, how to help, what to say—when in truth, more likely than not, just being ourselves and being present can make a difference, helping to color a moment, ease a worry, and lift a burden.

Don't hesitate to be yourself in those moments when you feel needed, rather than searching for the exact "right" phrase or action. More often than not, that unexpected offering that only you can provide is enough.

3 pounds russet or red
  potatoes, peeled and
  quartered

1 tablespoon salt, or more
  to taste

4 tablespoons unsalted
  butter

2 cups freshly grated
  cheddar cheese

½ cup sour cream

½ teaspoon nutmeg
  powder, or more to taste

*Ingredients continued on
  page 155*

**1.** Place the potatoes in a large pot and cover with enough cold water to rise 2 inches above the top of the potatoes.

**2.** Add 1 tablespoon salt to the water and bring to a boil.

**3.** Once boiling, cover and lower the heat to a simmer. Cook for about 20 minutes, until the potatoes are soft or a fork easily pierces through them.

**4.** Drain the potatoes, but don't rinse them, and then return them to the pot.

**5.** Begin to mash the potatoes using a potato masher or a fork. When they are about half mashed and still warm, add the butter and let it melt as you continue to mash.

½ teaspoon
 black pepper
½ teaspoon cayenne
 powder, or more to taste
½ cup heavy cream

**6.** Add the cheddar, sour cream, nutmeg, pepper, and cayenne and mix together with a wooden spoon or rubber spatula.

**7.** Add the heavy cream in small amounts until you reach your desired consistency.

**8.** Taste and add more salt, cayenne, or nutmeg if desired.

# Cauliflower Mashed Potatoes SERVES 6

A little healthy, a lot delicious, these potatoes are perfect when I want creamy, rich mashed potatoes but want to feel good about what I'm eating. While they have cauliflower in them, I wouldn't quite say they are *actually* healthy—though they do contain a vegetable, so there's that.

The ingredients, however, offer some serious power. Cauliflower calls forth the sense that we are of the moon, made of multitudes, while the potatoes ground us to the earth, a steady reflection of who we choose to be in this moment, in the here and now. Stars to reach for, roots to grow.

1 large head cauliflower, cut into small florets

2 tablespoons olive oil

½ teaspoon salt, or more to taste

½ teaspoon black pepper, or more to taste

2 pounds Yukon gold potatoes, peeled and diced into 1-inch pieces

3 tablespoons unsalted butter

6 garlic cloves, chopped

3 tablespoons sour cream

¼ cup Parmesan cheese

1 tablespoon minced fresh rosemary

½ teaspoon smoked paprika

**1.** Preheat your oven to 425°F.

**2.** Spread the cauliflower out on a baking sheet, drizzle with the olive oil, and toss to coat.

**3.** Season the cauliflower with the salt and pepper and toss again.

**4.** Spread the cauliflower florets into a single layer and bake for 15 to 20 minutes, or until your desired tenderness is reached and the florets are golden at the edges. The baking time may vary depending on the size of your pieces. Set the cauliflower aside.

**5.** Place the potatoes in a medium saucepan and cover with cold water. Bring to a boil over high heat. Once boiling, reduce the heat to medium and simmer until tender, about 18 minutes.

**6.** While the potatoes are cooking, heat the butter in a small pan set over medium-high heat.

**7.** Add the garlic to the pan and sauté until fragrant, approximately 1 minute.

**8.** Put the garlic butter and cauliflower into a food processor or blender and combine well.

**9.** Drain the potatoes and place them back into the pot.

**10.** Add the cauliflower mixture, sour cream, Parmesan, rosemary, and paprika. Using a potato masher or large spoon or fork, mash and combine all the ingredients.

**11.** Add salt and pepper to taste.

*cauliflower multitudes*

# Cheesy Grits SERVES 4

A break from potatoes as a side, grits provide a lovely alternative. These pair perfectly with shrimp or spiced chicken and can take an everyday meal and make it feel exceptional. And truth be told, they're a snap to make, so shoot for exceptional. Make the unexpected dish, take the less expected turn, find the fortuitous opportunity. You won't regret it.

2 cups chicken broth

2 cups water

1 cup traditional grits (not quick or instant)

½ teaspoon garlic powder

1 ½ cups shredded cheddar cheese

4 tablespoons unsalted butter

Splash of cream (optional)

**1.** In a medium saucepan set over high heat, combine the broth and water and bring to a boil.

**2.** Add the grits and garlic powder and lower the heat to a simmer. Continue to simmer, uncovered, for about 20 minutes, or until thick and creamy. (Check the grits' package directions for exact timing.)

**3.** Remove the grits from the heat and stir in the cheddar and butter until melted.

**4.** Add a splash of cream if desired.

**5.** Serve hot.

# Sweet Potato Fries SERVES 4

There's a serious and heated ongoing debate at my house over fries. Specifically, sweet potato fries. My daughter has her doubts over whether they are ever the appropriate side when "regular" fries might be available. However, over the years I feel like I've persuaded her a bit, or at least worn her down. I like to think sweet potato fries are the perfect accompaniment to a spicy meal, a great counterpoint to something smokey like chipotle. Like all potatoes, sweet ones offer grounding, but they are unique in their ability to encourage harmony and ignite friendship. None of these particular qualities are something I can point to as encouraging Samaire to eat my favorite version of fries more often, but perhaps it's what helps us meet in the middle.

3 tablespoons olive oil, and more for preparing the baking sheets

4 medium sweet potatoes

½ teaspoon fine sea salt

½ teaspoon black pepper

¼ teaspoon cayenne pepper

**1.** Preheat the oven to 450°F.

**2.** Lightly oil two baking sheets and place them into the oven to preheat.

**3.** Slice the sweet potatoes into 1/2-inch sticks. Slice in half first and then place the flat side down to avoid chasing after rolling and rocking potatoes with your knife.

**4.** Place the sweet potato sticks in a large bowl and toss with the olive oil, salt, pepper, and cayenne.

**5.** Remove the preheated baking sheets from the oven and carefully place the sweet potato sticks on them. Spread the fries out and try not to crowd them, or they won't develop the lovely crunchy outsides we all love. *A good lesson for all of us is that sometimes to develop into our best selves, we just need a little space.*

**6.** Place the baking sheets back in the oven and bake the fries for 10 minutes. (I often have to make these in batches because my oven is too small for 2 baking sheets.) At the 10-minute mark, turn the fries and rotate the pans, then bake for another 15 to 25 minutes. You will know the fries are ready to be taken out when their surface looks dry and puffed up a little. Don't fret if the edges turn brown; it's just the sugar in the potato caramelizing, and it'll be delectable.

sweet potato

grounding

# *Vie Bien-Aimée*
# BAKED GOODS

**THE POWER OF THE** unique magic behind our meals is beautifully apparent in freshly baked bread. The smell can bring us to a safe and warm moment almost instantly. But bread can be challenging and intimidating—a balancing act, a measured procedure, a tactile process. Making bread requires us to both (literally) dig in elbow-deep and to walk away. Mathematic procedure, chemical reaction, and a little bit of faith build the best of breads. Logic and love. Practice and perseverance.

Bread carries within it yeast and the energy of life. It is no coincidence that bread grounds us, that it brings us closer to ourselves, that it reflects the complexities and rewards of a life well-lived and well-loved—vie bien-aimée. So trust the process. Dig in with both hands. Make something truly delicious.

# Homemade Herb Loaf SERVES 6

This bread is made to share. Invite friends over and sit in the garden in the twilight of the evening, bake a loaf of bread, share a bottle of wine, and—if only for a moment—take the time to wish, to hope, that you will always be this happy, this healthy, and this blessed no matter the challenges headed your way. I wish that for you: endless evenings filled with promise.

2 cups warm water (not hot, but warmer than room temperature)

2 teaspoons sugar

1 ½ teaspoons (one ¼-ounce packet) dry yeast

4 cups unbleached all-purpose flour or bread flour

2 teaspoons kosher salt

Unsalted butter or cooking spray for greasing

*Ingredients continued on* *page 165*

**1.** Pour the warm water into a medium bowl, add the sugar, and stir to dissolve the sugar.

**2.** Pour the yeast into the sugar water and let it bloom, watching it bubble up and get foamy, then set aside. This is to see if your yeast will work. It's a great job to assign to small ones and fun to watch happen. If, for whatever reason, it doesn't bubble, then it's a good sign to start again with new yeast.

**3.** In another medium bowl, mix together the flour and salt.

**4.** Dig a well into the middle of the flour mixture and pour the yeasted sugar water into the well. Stir until the flour is no longer visible and is completely combined into the wet ingredients.

**5.** Place the dough into a lightly greased bowl.

**6.** Cover the bowl with a towel and let the dough rise in a warm space for at least 1 hour. It should just about double in size.

**7.** When about 45 minutes have passed, butter your baking container or spray with cooking spray. I usually bake this as one loaf in a Dutch oven, but it easily splits in half to make two loaves in regular-size loaf containers.

**FOR SERVING**

4 tablespoons unsalted
  butter, melted

Sea salt, to taste

2 tablespoons chopped
  fresh herbs of choice (such
  as thyme, sage, parsley, or
  oregano)

Olive oil for dipping

Wine for pairing (optional)

**8.** After an hour has passed, punch down your dough, then roll it into a round loaf, tucking the edges into the bottom sides of the dough, or use a pastry cutter or sharp knife to cut the dough into halves and roll into two loaves.

**9.** Place the dough into the prepared Dutch oven or baking pans.

**10.** Let the dough rise again for about 30 minutes, until it is just above the top of your pan(s).

**11.** Preheat your oven to 450°F. *At this point, I like to take small pieces of dough to create designs on the top of the loaf or use a knife to carve simple symbols. It adds a bit of interest and is a reminder that this loaf is something special. As you place the decorations on top of the loaf, imagine how you hope this loaf makes those who consume it feel. Concentrate on the intention you wish to imbue. Gently and purposefully cut the dough or place the designs.*

**12.** Bake for 15 minutes, then reduce the oven temperature to 350°F and bake for 20 minutes longer.

**13.** Remove the bread from the oven and brush melted butter over the top, sprinkling with sea salt and fresh herbs. *The herbs can be anything that are in season or handily close by. You can choose them for what they stand for: thyme for courage in facing transitions, sage for purity, parsley for transitions, oregano for joy. This is a bread for meeting challenges with fervor and happiness, for bravery in the face of change. After all, we reap what we sow, and bringing joyful energy to transitions will beget joyful outcomes.*

**14.** Dip your bread into delicious olive oil, providing fruitfulness and security, and toast with a glass of wine. Wish for those around you that the nourishment and happiness they're experiencing right now may follow them always.

# Focaccia SERVES 10 TO 12

Focaccia is yet another dish that always sounded fancy to me but is so very easy to make. Even better? It can be tailored to fit any flavor profile and to suit any occasion.

2 tablespoons unsalted
  butter or baking spray

5 tablespoons olive oil,
  divided, and more for
  topping

1 ½ cups warm water

2 teaspoons sugar

1 ¼ tablespoons instant
  yeast

3 ½ to 3 ¾ cups all-purpose
  flour

2 teaspoons salt, and more
  to taste

**FOR TOPPING**

Fresh herbs of choice

Black pepper

Roasted vegetables
  (optional)

Grated cheese of choice
  (optional)

**1.** Lightly grease a 9-by-13-inch baking sheet with the butter. If you'd rather not use butter, a good dose of baking spray will work just as well.

**2.** Drizzle 2 tablespoons of the olive oil over the butter or spray. The butter keeps the bread from sticking and the oil gives your bread that yummy crispy bottom.

**3.** Combine the water and sugar in a small bowl, then pour the yeast over it and let it bloom, bubbling up and getting foamy.

**4.** While the yeast blooms, combine 3 1/2 cups flour, the remaining 3 tablespoons olive oil, and the salt in a large bowl. Make a small well in the middle of the mixture and add the water-yeast-sugar mixture to the well.

**5.** With a Danish dough whisk or large wooden spoon, mix the yeast mixture into the flour mixture until the dough begins to combine and pull away from the sides of the bowl.

**6.** Now use your hands to begin to work the dough until it's completely combined, kneading gently for 3 to 5 minutes. The dough will be sticky but will become less sticky as you work it. Spray your hands with baking spray to help prevent the dough from sticking to them, or run them quickly under water to dampen them. If you really need to, add a bit of flour—but avoid adding too much; try to stick to no more than 1/4 cup.

**7.** Place the dough into the center of your pan and use your palms to flatten it into a rectangle. Then stretch it gently to the edges of the pan. You may have to hold it in place for a count of 15 seconds to get it to stay where you need it.

**8.** Cover the dough and let it rise for 1 hour. It should get puffy, but don't expect it to double in size.

**9.** About 45 minutes into the rising, preheat your oven to 375°F.

**10.** Once the dough has risen, poke the dough all over with the tips of your fingers. *This is arguably the best part of this process. It's admittedly weirdly satisfying and always reminds me of playing with clay or in the sand as a kid. I recommend you savor this moment. Don't hurry through to just get it done. Instead make a pattern, make chaos. Fire up your inner child and be tactile and present. We don't get enough time to just play.*

**11.** Top the dough with olive oil, herbs, salt, and pepper, or any delicious toppings of your choice. Roasted veggies and cheeses are a surefire win.

**12.** Bake the bread for 25 to 30 minutes, or until golden.

**13.** Remove the bread from the oven and let rest for 5 minutes. Lift it out of its pan and onto a large cutting board before serving.

## CARROT FETA FOCACCIA

SERVES 10 TO 12

Carrots imbue confidence and creativity and remind us that there is fun to be had in simply being ourselves. With slivers of almonds sprinkled on top, this dish is designed to bring you the kind of prosperity that comes with letting your whole self shine. It is great for a night leading up to a full moon or big meeting, or a day when you need a small boost of confidence and self-love.

2 tablespoons unsalted butter or cooking spray

5 tablespoons olive oil, divided, and more for topping

2 teaspoons sugar

1 ¼ tablespoons instant yeast

3 ½ cups all-purpose flour

2 teaspoons salt

3 carrots (preferably multicolored *because I like pretty things!*)

¾ cup slivered almonds

½ cup crumbled feta cheese

Hot Honey (see page 267), to taste

**1.** Using the butter, olive oil, sugar, yeast, flour, and salt, follow the directions for the Focaccia on page xx through step 10.

**2.** While the dough is rising, use a peeler to remove the outer skin of the carrots and discard this layer. Then peel the rest of the carrots to create thin ribbons.

**3.** Once you've poked holes across the risen dough, scatter the carrot ribbons, almonds, and feta evenly across the bread. Drizzle with olive oil.

**4.** Bake the bread at 375°F until it's golden, 25 to 30 minutes.

**5.** Remove the bread from the oven and let it rest for 5 minutes. Lift it out of its pan and onto a large cutting board and drizzle with Hot Honey before serving.

almonds

sense of purpose

## POTATO PANCETTA FOCACCIA

SERVES 10 TO 12

I know it's not shocking that potatoes ground us. Like all root vegetables, they provide a connection to the earth, within the darkness, and all that holds us steady in winds of change. There's a certain mystical feeling to the idea of holding fast within the dark, of recognizing that that is where so much growth happens—in the dark of the new moon, under the deep richness of the soil, beneath a mother's heart. We fear the idea of darkness so often, recoiling from the feeling of not knowing what might be next and of not seeing the path clearly. And yet, it is often in that darkness that we find a new path, a new way to approach something, a chance to stop and rest, to breathe and gain strength for what lies ahead—no matter what that is. This is the message held in a simple, brown potato, and this Potato Pancetta Focaccia is a dish to bake when you feel "in-between" and need to root yourself in the moment, rather than drifting between what has been and what might be. It is a reminder that here and now, wherever and however that may be, can be an opportunity. Or, you know, it's just a potato and this is just focaccia. Either way, this dish is pretty delicious.

1 garlic bulb

6 tablespoons olive oil, divided, and more for roasting the garlic and for topping

2 teaspoons salt, and more for roasting the garlic

Black pepper, to taste

½ pound pancetta, finely diced

*Ingredients continued on page 172*

**1.** Preheat your oven to 400°F.

**2.** Remove and throw away the papery outer skin from the bulb of garlic, leaving the skins on that cover the individual cloves. Cut the top 1/4 to 1/2 inch off the cloves, cutting off the pointy parts and exposing their tops.

**3.** Place the cloves on a sheet of aluminum foil, pour olive oil over them, and generously cover with salt and pepper. Pull the corners of the foil up and wrap them together so the garlic is completely enclosed.

**4.** Roast the garlic in the oven for 40 minutes. Once the garlic is roasted, let it cool. When it's cool to the touch, hold the bulbs over a bowl or jar and squeeze

1 ½ pounds russet potatoes, diced small

2 tablespoons unsalted butter or cooking spray

2 teaspoons sugar

1 ¼ tablespoons instant yeast

3 ½ cups all-purpose flour

2 ½ tablespoons finely chopped fresh rosemary leaves

the garlic out of the bulbs. They should be soft and fall right out. This roasting can be done ahead of time, and you can store the roasted garlic in a jar for a couple of days until you're ready to use it.

**5.** Set a small skillet over medium heat and cook the pancetta in 1 tablespoon olive oil until cooked through and crisp, about 5 minutes. Once cooked, place it on a plate lined with a paper towel.

**6.** Place the diced potatoes in a pot. Fill the pot with cold water until the water rises 2 inches above the potato pieces.

**7.** Salt the water, bring it to a boil, and cook the potatoes at a boil for 10 minutes, or until tender. Drain the potatoes.

**8.** Gently fold the pancetta and at least 4 cloves of the roasted garlic into the potatoes, doing your best not to mash them. If you like, you can add more garlic to taste. (I usually use the whole bulb!). Set the potatoes aside. *Garlic and pancetta round out this bread to offer protection and patience in uncertain times, while rosemary gives us the strength of all we have been through and all who have come before us.*

**9.** Using the butter, remaining 5 tablespoons olive oil, sugar, yeast, flour, and 2 teaspoons salt, follow the directions for the Focaccia on page 167 through step 10.

**10.** Spoon the potato mixture across the top of the bread in the pan.

**11.** Sprinkle rosemary over the mixture, then drizzle olive oil over all of it.

**12.** Bake the bread until it's golden, 25 to 30 minutes.

**13.** Remove the bread from the oven and let rest for 5 minutes. Lift it out of its pan and onto a large cutting board before serving.

## ZUCCHINI LEEK FOCACCIA

SERVES 10 TO 12

Zucchini are found during the first harvest festivals of the fall, making this a celebratory dish honoring the culmination of a season's hard work. Tenacious, they represent the ability to get the hard work done and offer a chance to look back at how you got to where you are. This is an opportunity to peel back the layers of all that went into your journey, to recognize all that you have striven for, all the late nights and early mornings, and to accept a moment to stand still, if only to catch a breath and revel in the outcome.

2 zucchini

8 tablespoons olive oil, divided, and more for drizzling the zucchini

1 tablespoon salt, divided, and more for seasoning the zucchini

1 teaspoon black pepper, and more for seasoning the zucchini

1 cup sliced leeks

2 tablespoons unsalted butter or cooking spray

2 teaspoons sugar

1 ¼ tablespoons instant yeast

3 ½ cups all-purpose flour

½ cup grated Parmesan cheese

1 ½ teaspoons flake salt

**1.** Preheat your oven to 450°F.

**2.** Slice the zucchini as thinly as you can. Place the slices on a baking sheet and drizzle olive oil, salt, and pepper over the zucchini.

**3.** Roast the zucchini until it starts to brown at the edges, 3 to 5 minutes. Some edges may get crispy. Set aside.

**4.** Heat 3 tablespoons of the olive oil in a small skillet set over medium-high heat.

**5.** Toss in the leeks and cook, stirring occasionally, until just soft. Set the cooked leeks aside.

**6.** Using the butter, remaining 5 tablespoons olive oil, sugar, yeast, flour, and 2 teaspoons salt, follow the directions for the Focaccia on page 167 through step 10.

**7.** Layer the slices of zucchini on the dough, then sprinkle on the leeks, Parmesan, flake salt, remaining 1 teaspoon salt, and black pepper. I like to make rows of my sliced zucchini, but if you aren't particular about how the slices lie, you can toss all of the toppings on at once.

**8.** Bake the bread until it's golden, 25 to 30 minutes.

**9.** Remove the bread from the oven and let rest for 5 minutes. Lift it out of its pan and onto a large cutting board before serving.

**LIGHT, FIRE, AND ABUNDANCE**

# Roasted Garlic Brioche Rolls SERVES 8 TO 10

Soft and buttery, these rolls not only taste heavenly but will fill your home with the rich and lovely aromas of roasted garlic and homemade bread. I sometimes make them just for that. They are perfect for rounding out a pasta and salad but wonderful alongside anything, honestly.

2 garlic bulbs

Olive oil, for roasting the garlic

2 ½ to 3 cups all-purpose flour, and more for flouring the work surface

2 ½ teaspoons instant yeast

1 ½ cups grated Parmesan cheese

1 tablespoon and ½ teaspoon garlic powder, divided

2 tablespoons and 1 teaspoon chopped fresh parsley, divided, and more for garnishing

¾ teaspoon salt, divided

⅔ cup whole milk, warm

2 tablespoons honey

3 eggs, divided

2 tablespoons unsalted butter, melted, and more for serving

½ cup (1 stick) unsalted butter, room temperature, and more for greasing the pan

**1.** Remove and throw away the papery outer skin from the garlic bulbs, leaving the skins on that cover the individual cloves. Cut the top 1/4 to 1/2 inch off the cloves, cutting off the pointy parts and exposing their tops.

**2.** Place the cloves on a sheet of aluminum foil and pour olive oil over them. Pull the corners of the foil up and wrap them together so the garlic is completely enclosed.

**3.** Roast the garlic in the oven for 40 minutes, then squeeze the cloves out of the papery skins and smash the cloves. This roasting can be done ahead of time, and you can store the roasted garlic in a jar for a couple of days until you're ready to use it.

**4.** In a large bowl, combine 2 1/2 cups flour with the yeast, Parmesan, 1 tablespoon garlic powder, 1 teaspoon parsley, and 1/2 teaspoon salt.

**5.** In a separate bowl, whisk together the warm milk, honey, 2 eggs, and melted butter.

**6.** Using a wooden spoon or Danish dough whisk, mix the dry and wet ingredients together completely, then knead for 4 to 5 minutes. If the dough seems sticky, add the remaining 1/2 cup of flour 1 tablespoon at a time.

**7.** Cover the bowl and let the dough sit at room temperature for 45 minutes. Give it another 15 minutes if it hasn't quite doubled.

**8.** While the dough rises, mix together the room-temperature butter, roasted garlic, remaining 2 tablespoons parsley, 1/4 teaspoon salt, and remaining 1/2 teaspoon garlic powder.

**9.** Place the garlic butter mix in the refrigerator to store until needed. This is an easy item to make ahead, but you will want to bring the garlic butter to room temperature before using so it's easy to spread it across the dough. If using right away, it's safe to keep on the counter; just keep it away from heat sources so it doesn't melt.

**10.** Preheat your oven to 450°F. Lightly grease a 5-by-9-inch loaf pan or 8-inch round cake pan.

**11.** When the dough has doubled in size, punch it down and turn it out onto a lightly floured work surface.

**12.** Shape the dough into a ball using your hands, then flatten it into a rectangle and roll it out until it is approximately 12 by 18 inches, keeping one of the long sides closest to you.

**13.** Generously spread the garlic butter over the dough, leaving a small border clear around the edges. *The garlic and parsley in the garlic butter offer protection, deterrence, an easing of whatever can weigh you down, and support against the depths to which it could take you.*

**14.** Beginning with the long edge of dough closest to you, roll the dough into a log, gently but tightly. Pinch the final edges of the dough to seal the seams of the rolls.

**15.** With a pastry cutter, sharp knife, or unflavored floss (that's right!), cut the log into 8 rolls. Arrange the rolls in the prepared pan, leaving enough room in the pan to avoid crowding, though as the rolls rise their sides will eventually touch.

**16.** Cover the dough and let rise for about 20 minutes in a room-temperature spot away from drafts.

**17.** In a small dish, beat the remaining egg with about a tablespoon of water to use as an egg wash. After the rise, brush the tops of the rolls with your egg wash.

**18.** Bake the rolls until they are browned on top, approximately 20 minutes.

**19.** Reduce the oven temperature to 350°F and bake another 25 to 30 minutes.

**20.** Remove the rolls from oven, top with additional melted butter, sprinkle parsley over the top, and serve warm.

# Zambrano Rolls (Cheddar and Jalapeño) SERVES 8 TO 10

I wish there were a moment I could point to when I knew Eliana and I would be true, lasting friends. Did her place in my heart first form when I realized that she was one of the few moms at drop-off and pick-up that I didn't feel horribly inept around? Or when I found out that she traveled with her daughter the same way we did with ours, far and with abandon? Maybe, and most likely, it took shape when we sat in the back row of the auditorium at school during the parents' sex-ed prep meeting, endlessly smirking over the fact that the principal seemed just as awkward and embarrassed over the subject matter as the eleven-year-olds she was about to teach.

I'm not fully sure when my feelings toward Eliana first formed, but I know how lucky Sam and I are to have Hugo and Eliana as stalwart companions on this journey of parenthood. They are the parents of our daughter's first first-grade friend, and have long since become family. Today, they are friends to commiserate and celebrate with on the daily. Over the years we have shared innumerable adventures, and I always look forward to the next one.

Cheese often symbolizes transformation and a view of what's to come, while jalapeños amplify courage and help deter evil. I can't help but think those are also qualities we find in the best of friends, people who witness and support us as we evolve into who we hope to be and who give us courage to keep at it even when times are rough. I hope you are blessed with a multitude of such people in your lives too.

2 ½ to 3 cups all-purpose flour, and more for flouring the work surface

¼ cup cheddar cheese powder

Ingredients continued on page 182

**1.** In a large bowl, combine 2 1/2 cups flour with the cheddar powder, yeast, and salt.

**2.** In a separate bowl, whisk together the warm milk, 2 eggs, 2 tablespoons jalapeño brine, the honey, and melted butter.

**3.** Using a wooden spoon or Danish dough whisk, mix the dry and wet ingredients together completely, then knead for 4 to 5 minutes. If the dough seems

2 ¼ teaspoons instant yeast

½ teaspoon salt

⅔ cup whole milk, warm

3 eggs, divided

¼ cup and 2 tablespoons
  jalapeño brine, divided

2 tablespoons honey

2 tablespoons unsalted
  butter, melted

8 ounces cream cheese,
  room temperature

2 ½ cups shredded cheddar
  cheese

7 to 8 jalapeños, seeded
  and chopped

Olive oil for cooking

Pickled jalapeños for
  garnishing

sticky, add the remaining 1/2 cup of flour 1 tablespoon at a time.

**4.** Cover the dough and let it sit at room temperature for 45 minutes. Give it another 15 minutes if it hasn't quite doubled.

**5.** In a medium bowl, use a spoon to combine the cream cheese, cheddar, chopped jalapeños, and remaining 1/4 cup jalapeño brine. Store in a cool place—room temperature is fine; you want the cream cheese to stay soft but not melt.

**6.** Preheat your oven to 450°F. Grease a 5-by-9-inch loaf or round cake pan with the oil.

**7.** When the dough has doubled in size, punch it down and turn it out onto a lightly floured work surface.

**8.** Shape the dough into a ball using your hands, then flatten it into a rectangle and roll it out until it is approximately 12 by 18 inches, making sure one of the long ends is closest to you.

**9.** Generously spread the cream cheese mixture over the dough, leaving about an inch margin and not covering the edges of the dough.

**10.** Beginning with the long edge of dough closest to you, roll the dough into a log, gently but tightly. Be sure to seal the final edge by pinching it slightly with the body of the log roll.

**11.** With a pastry cutter, sharp knife, or unflavored floss, cut the log into 8 rolls, pinching one end to seal. Arrange the rolls in the prepared pan, leaving

enough room in the pan to avoid crowding, though as the rolls rise their sides will eventually touch.

**12.** Cover the dough and let it rise for about 20 minutes in a room-temperature place away from drafts. I tend to keep mine in our hallway away from the heat of the oven and the seasonally cool space in front of our windows.

**13.** Beat the remaining egg with 1 tablespoon of water in a small dish to use as an egg wash. After the rise, brush the tops of the rolls with your egg wash.

**14.** Bake the rolls until browned on top, approximately 20 minutes.

**15.** Reduce the oven temperature to 350°F and bake another 25 to 30 minutes.

**16.** Remove the rolls from the oven, garnish with the pickled jalapeños, and serve warm.

# Sausage Pesto Rolls SERVES 8 TO 10

These rolls are a meal unto themselves. Packed with pesto and sausage, they are perfect when topped with a little Hot Honey (see page 267) and served alongside a salad. However, you can fill them with just about anything: Bolognese Sauce (see page 273) and mozzarella; taco meat, enchilada sauce, and shredded cheese—it's all up for grabs. Find your favorite flavors and roll 'em up! Then head out to the park, drive-in, or even your couch, and enjoy some of the best comfort food around.

2 ½ to 3 cups all-purpose flour, and more for flouring the work surface

1 ½ cups grated Parmesan cheese

2 ½ teaspoons instant yeast

½ teaspoon salt

⅔ cup whole milk, warm

3 eggs, divided

2 tablespoons unsalted butter, melted

1 tablespoon honey

Cooking spray

2 cups Kale Pumpkin Seed Pesto (see page 278) or other pesto

½ pound sweet or hot Italian sausage, crumbled

Habanero Hot Honey (see page 269), to taste

**1.** In a large bowl, combine 2 1/2 cups flour with the Parmesan, yeast, and salt.

**2.** In a separate bowl, whisk together the warm milk, 2 eggs, the melted butter, and honey.

**3.** Using a wooden spoon or Danish dough whisk, mix the dry and wet ingredients together completely, then knead for 4 to 5 minutes. If the dough seems sticky, add the remaining 1/2 cup flour 1 tablespoon at a time.

**4.** Cover the dough and let it sit at room temperature for 45 minutes. Give it another 15 minutes if it hasn't quite doubled.

**5.** Preheat your oven to 450°F, and grease a 5-by-9-inch loaf pan or an 8-inch round cake pan with cooking spray.

**6.** When the dough has doubled in size, punch it down and turn it out onto a lightly floured work surface. Shape it into a ball using your hands, then flatten it into a rectangle and roll it out until it is approximately 12 by 18 inches, making sure one of the long sides is closest to you.

**7.** Generously spread the pesto over the dough, leaving about an inch clear around the edges.

**8.** Top the pesto with the sausage.

**9.** Beginning with the long edge of dough closest to you, roll the dough into a log, gently but tightly.

**10.** With a pastry cutter, sharp knife, or unflavored floss, cut the log into 8 rolls. Arrange the rolls in the prepared pan, leaving enough room in the pan to avoid crowding, though as the rolls rise their sides will eventually touch.

**11.** Cover and let rise for about 20 minutes in a warm place. At room temperature is fine; just be sure it's nowhere near drafts of cool air.

**12.** Beat the remaining egg with 1 tablespoon water in a small dish to use as an egg wash.

**13.** After the rise, brush the tops of the rolls with your egg wash.

**14.** Bake until browned on top, approximately 20 minutes.

**15.** Reduce the oven temperature to 350°F and bake another 25 to 30 minutes.

**16.** Remove the rolls from the oven, drizzle with Habanero Hot Honey, and serve warm.

# Parker Rolls SERVES 6

I experienced my toughest year in 2014. It was filled with broken bones and what at the time felt like insurmountable challenges. But on January 13, 2014, before my awesome run of bad luck, I spent a wonderful night making Parker Rolls with my daughter. She was studying how bread was made in school, so we decided to make some at home. We spent an amazing evening rolling dough, watching it rise, and then baking it to golden perfection.

It wasn't a lost year. It was filled with small moments of sheer joy. These rolls remind me to take those moments as they come, to be present for them, to pause to enjoy them, and to allow them to help carry me through all the moments that may come between.

6 tablespoons salted butter, melted and cooled to room temperature

3 tablespoons honey

1 ½ cups milk

½ cup (1 stick) unsalted butter, chopped, and more for greasing the bowl

½ cup sugar

½ cup warm water

2 tablespoons active dry yeast

3 eggs

1 ½ teaspoons salt, and more for serving

6 cups all-purpose flour, and more for flouring the work surface

**1.** In a small bowl, combine the melted salted butter and the honey and mix with a fork until well combined.

**2.** Place the honey butter in the refrigerator to store until needed. This is easy to make ahead, but you will want to bring it to room temperature before using so it's easy to spread across the dough. If using right away, it's safe to keep on the counter; just keep it away from heat sources so it doesn't melt.

**3.** Heat the milk in a small saucepan set over medium heat to bring to a simmer. Once simmering, remove it from the heat and stir in the unsalted butter and sugar. Let cool.

**4.** Dissolve the yeast in the warm water and let sit until foamy.

**5.** Combine the milk mixture, yeast mixture, eggs, salt, and 3 cups of the flour in a large bowl or the bowl of a stand mixer with a dough hook attachment.

Mix with a Danish dough whisk or the dough hook until well combined and smooth.

**6.** Add the remaining flour 1/2 cup at a time until a smooth ball forms. You may not need all the flour.

**7.** Once the dough is smooth, place it on a lightly floured surface and knead by hand for another 5 minutes.

**8.** Place the dough in a lightly greased bowl, cover, and let rise at room temperature, away from any drafts, for about 1 hour or until it doubles in size.

**9.** Once the dough has risen, punch it down in the bowl. *Sometimes despite finding the joy, it feels nice to punch something. So go for it!*

**10.** Place the dough back on a lightly floured surface and divide it into 6 pieces. Roll each in your palm to form balls.

**11.** Set the dough balls onto a parchment-lined baking sheet, cover, and let rise for another 35 minutes.

**12.** Preheat your oven to 350°F.

**13.** Uncover the dough and bake it for 20 minutes, or until golden brown.

**14.** Remove the dough from the oven, brush it with the melted honey butter, and sprinkle lightly with salt before serving.

# Pizza

Pizza is wonderfully customizable. It can be loaded with all kinds of meats, piled with every veggie imaginable, or profoundly simple. It can also be sweet or savory, deep dish or thin crust. It is one of the easiest recipes to make our own and modify to suit our purpose. It's a nice way to experiment or just clean out the fridge. Either way, it's a wonderful opportunity to have some fun and be truly present to build an intentional meal that feeds your soul and nourishes your heart.

## DELICIOUS DOUGH

MAKES THREE 12-INCH PIZZAS

This dough will make three 12-inch pizzas using a 12-inch pizza pan, or you can use 8-inch cake pans or pie plates to make four individual pizzas. You can also use this dough in a cast-iron pan to make deep-dish pizzas.

2 cups warm water

2 tablespoons active yeast

4 to 5 cups all-purpose flour, and more for coating the bowl

1 tablespoon sugar

1 tablespoon salt

2 tablespoons Italian seasoning

2 tablespoons olive oil (see Tip), and more for greasing the pans

**1.** Make sure your water is slightly warmer than room temperature, but not hot—you'll know it's perfectly lukewarm when you can dip your finger into the water and it feels neither cooler nor warmer—and sprinkle the yeast in. Let bloom to bubble and foam.

**2.** In a large bowl, combine 4 cups flour with the sugar, salt, and Italian seasoning.

**3.** Add the oil and the yeast mixture to the center of the bowl, then use a Danish dough whisk to mix everything together into a mostly cohesive ball of dough. This will take a few minutes, and it will be sticky.

**4.** Lightly flour the inside of a large shallow bowl, transfer the dough to it, and begin to knead the dough in the floured bowl. Add flour as needed until the dough is smooth instead of sticky, using up to the full remaining cup of flour if necessary. You may find you don't need the whole cup. After kneading the dough for 7 minutes, shape it into a smooth ball.

**5.** Cover the dough and let it rise at room temperature for 45 minutes to 1 hour. Once risen, punch down the dough. *This can be outrageously satisfying. Go for it!*

**6.** Preheat your oven to 450°F and lightly grease whatever size pans you are using.

**7.** Separate the dough according to how many pizzas you want to make and begin to work the dough. Start by holding up the dough and slowly turning it in the air, stretching it out horizontally as gravity pulls it vertically.

**8.** When you get the dough stretched out, place it in the pan or pans and begin to work it toward the edges, trying to keep the thickness as consistent as possible. *The dough has a "memory" and will fight you a bit as you stretch it. Be patient. Work the dough to where you would like it to be and just hold it there a moment, counting to five. Work your way around the pan or pans in this manner, patiently easing the dough into the shape you wish. Remind yourself as you work the dough, easing it out and holding it in place, of how you can exercise the same patience in other areas of your life, slowly working your way to where and how you want to be.*

**9.** The dough is now ready to be baked with your favorite ingredients for 12 to 15 minutes to make a pizza that should come off of the pan fairly easy to cut. *Resist the urge to eat right away. Let the pizza cool and avoid that annoying burn on the roof of your mouth. My family is never quite able to wait, but I have hope for you!*

## Tip

If you have garlic oil on hand, you can use that in place of the olive oil. For a slightly sweet crust, replace 1 tablespoon of the olive oil with 1 tablespoon honey. If you'd like to make the dough ahead of time, you have two amazing options. You can let the dough rise, deflate it, then cover it and put it in the fridge overnight, and the next day stretch it into your chosen pan and allow it to come to room temperature before topping and enjoying. Or if you're super ahead of the game, you can make the crust and freeze it for up to 3 months. Follow the instructions, but instead of topping your pizza dough in the pan, go ahead and place it straight in the oven. Bake it until it just firms up (when you poke your finger into it there's no permanent mark, or until the edges are just starting to become golden, about 8 minutes for a thin-crusted pizza, 10 minutes for "hand-tossed" thickness, or 12 minutes for a deep dish). Then remove the pizza and let it cool completely before wrapping it tightly and freezing it. When you're ready to use it, take it out of the freezer and let it come to room temperature. Top it with all your favorite items and bake until all the topping are cooked through and the cheese is melted. Bon appétit, you super planner!

## WHITE PIZZA

FOSTERS TRUST IN ONESELF, PROTECTION OF YOUR OWN GROWTH AND TRANSFORMATION

1 recipe Delicious Dough
 (see page 191)

3 cups ricotta cheese

4 cloves garlic, roasted and
 smashed

2 cups shredded mozzarella
 cheese

1 cup shredded Parmesan
 cheese

½ pound broccolini,
 chopped

**1.** Mix the ricotta and roasted garlic together and spread over the dough.

**2.** Sprinkle the mozzarella, Parmesan, and broccolini over the top.

**3.** Bake at 450°F for 12 to 15 minutes.

## HOT HONEY PIZZA

OPENS HEARTS AND MINDS TO RECEIVE GENEROSITY AND LOVE AND SAVOR THE SWEETNESS OF THOSE GIFTS

1 recipe Delicious Dough
 (see page 191)

2 cups Simple Marinara (see
 page 270)

2 cups shredded mozzarella

3 ounces soppressata, sliced

Hot Honey (see page 267)
 or your favorite store-
 bought spicy honey (we
 like habanero-chili honey),
 for drizzling

**1.** Spread the marinara over the dough.

**2.** Sprinkle the mozzarella over the marinara and place the soppressata over the mozzarella.

**3.** Bake at 450°F for 12 to 15 minutes.

**4.** Remove the pizza from the oven and drizzle with Hot Honey.

## SAUSAGE AND PEPPER PIZZA

UNCOVERS THE POSSIBILITIES OF DESIRE AND LOVE

1 recipe Delicious Dough
(see page 191)

2 cups Spicy Arrabbiata
Sauce (see page 271)

2 green bell peppers, diced

1 pound Italian sausage, cut
into bite-size pieces

1 red onion, diced

1 cup shredded pecorino
cheese, and more for
topping

2 cups shredded mozzarella
cheese

**1.** Spread the Spicy Arrabbiata Sauce over the dough.

**2.** Sprinkle the peppers, sausage, and onion across the sauce.

**3.** Spread the cheeses over the vegetables and sausage.

**4.** Bake at 450°F for 12 to 15 minutes.

**5.** Remove the pizza from the oven and sprinkle with extra pecorino.

## BBQ CHICKEN PIZZA

IMBUES INSIGHT AND CLARITY AND INCREASES COURAGE ABOUT WHAT MAY BE NEXT.

1 recipe Delicious Dough
(see page 191)

2 cups BBQ Sauce (see
page 283)

1 (approximately 2-pound)
rotisserie chicken,
shredded

2 green bell peppers,
chopped

1 red onion, diced

2 cups shredded white
cheddar cheese

1 cup sweet corn

2 jalapeños, seeded
and diced

**1.** Spread the BBQ Sauce over the dough and top with the chicken.

**2.** Sprinkle the green bell peppers and onion over the chicken.

**3.** Spread the cheddar over the peppers, onion, and chicken.

**4.** Top with sweet corn and jalapeños.

**5.** Bake at 450°F for 12 to 15 minutes.

*Tip*
..........................................

This makes a great
deep-dish pizza.

# Cinnamon Rolls

I'll be the first to admit that in a pinch I reach for the canned cinnamon rolls. You know the ones, with the little tubs of icing at the end. But while their can makes a very satisfying pop when you open it, they cannot compare to fresh, homemade rolls right out of the oven. There's just something especially comforting and warming about digging into a homemade roll dripping with icing and served right out of its pan. Not to mention the amazing fragrance that fills your home. To me, it's a vital part of the whole experience: seeing my kids come out from their rooms, out of their books and games, with expectant smiles, lured by the amazing aroma of freshly baked cinnamon rolls—that's a hell of an allurement spell right there.

Cinnamon roll recipes can seem intimidating, but hang in there—they are super hard to mess up. And once you have the process down, you can add any number of new flavors and fillings to create your own special deliciously concocted roll. You just need to be patient with yourself and trust the process. (That's my personal struggle; I speak from experience!) If you take your time and relish each step, the end result is one to be savored by you and about ten of your friends. (Or, you know, just by you, ten to twelve times.)

## CLASSIC CINNAMON ROLLS

SERVES 10

The warmth of cinnamon can't help but warm your heart, and those of everyone you may share these with, of course.

### DOUGH

½ cup whole milk, room temperature, and ⅔ cup whole milk, cold

Ingredients continued on page 199

**1.** Combine 1/2 cup room-temperature whole milk and 3 tablespoons bread flour in a small pot and stir until there are no lumps.

**2.** Place the pot over medium heat and cook, stirring regularly, for 1 to 3 minutes. You will know it has thickened to the right consistency when your spoon

2 ½ cups and 3 tablespoons
  bread flour, and more for
  flouring the work surface

2 tablespoons sugar

2 ½ teaspoons instant yeast

1 teaspoon salt

4 tablespoons unsalted
  butter, softened, and more
  for greasing the bowl and
  plastic wrap

**FILLING**

2 tablespoons unsalted
  butter, melted

1 packed cup dark brown
  sugar

2 tablespoons bread flour

2 tablespoons cinnamon
  powder

1 teaspoon nutmeg powder

A pinch of salt

*Ingredients continued on
  page 200*

leaves a clean trail in the mixture when it is dragged along the bottom of the pan.

**3.** Transfer the hot flour mixture to a large bowl or stand mixer fitted with a dough hook attachment.

**4.** Add 2/3 cup cold milk straight out of the fridge, then add the remaining bread flour, the sugar, yeast, and salt.

**5.** Mix steadily to bring the dough together. I use a Danish dough whisk, or even a wooden spoon. Eventually as the dough gets thicker, I will just use my hands until the ingredients are all well combined and begin to form a solid mass. If using a mixer, stop mixing as soon as the dough begins to pull away from the sides of the bowl. Then knead the dough by hand for about 15 minutes, until the dough is smooth, elastic, and tacky.

**6.** Shape the dough into a ball, place it in a lightly greased bowl, and cover.

**7.** Let the dough rise for 60 to 90 minutes, or until puffy. It's okay if it does not double in size.

**8.** While the dough is rising, make the filling: place the melted butter in a medium bowl and add the remaining ingredients, stirring until the mixture is the texture of damp sand.

**9.** Line a baking sheet with parchment paper.

**10.** Transfer the dough to a lightly floured work surface and press it into a 10-by-12-inch rectangle that's about 1/2 inch thick.

**11.** Place the filling onto the dough, covering all but a 1/2-inch strip along one long side.

## CREAM CHEESE ICING

8 ounces cream cheese, softened (brick-style, not spreadable)

½ cup (1 stick) unsalted butter

2 tablespoons vanilla extract

¼ teaspoon salt

4 cups powdered sugar

**12.** Starting with the filling-covered long side, roll the dough gently but tightly.

**13.** Using a pastry cutter, sharp knife, or unflavored floss, cut the roll into 1 1/2- to 2-inch sections. Place the rolls onto the prepared baking sheet.

**14.** Cover the rolls with lightly greased plastic wrap and let them rise for 30 to 60 minutes. You will know they are done when the dough doesn't bounce back immediately if you press it with your finger.

**15.** Place a rack in the top third of your oven if possible, then preheat your oven to 375°F.

**16.** Bake the rolls until they're a light golden brown, 14 to 18 minutes.

**17.** Remove the rolls from the oven and top with the butter. Let cool for 10 to 15 minutes.

**18.** To make the icing, combine all the ingredients except the powdered sugar in a medium mixing bowl and beat with a mixer or by hand (I find a heavy fork, whisk, or Danish dough whisk works well) until creamy, well combined, and lump-free.

**19.** Add the powdered sugar gradually (too much at once will send it everywhere!) until completely combined.

**20.** Once the rolls are cool, spread the icing generously across the cinnamon rolls.

intuition

cinnamon

# CHERRY LEMON ROLLS

SERVES 10

Ah, cherries, to remind us that while our time may be short, we can make it glorious. It's easiest to buy cherry pie filling in a can and I certainly won't fault you for doing so, but if you're feeling like homemade is the way to go, use the recipe here to add a special touch.

## DOUGH

½ cup whole milk, room temperature, and ⅔ cup whole milk, cold

2 ½ cups and 3 tablespoons bread flour, and more for flouring the work surface

1 tablespoon lemon juice

2 tablespoons sugar

1 tablespoon lemon zest

2 ½ teaspoons instant yeast

1 teaspoon salt

4 tablespoons unsalted butter, softened, and more for greasing the bowl and plastic wrap

## FILLING

4 ounces cream cheese, room temperature

*Ingredients continued on page 202*

**1.** Combine 1/2 cup room-temperature whole milk and 3 tablespoons bread flour in a small pot and stir until there are no lumps.

**2.** Place the pot over medium heat, add the lemon juice, and cook, stirring regularly, for 1 to 3 minutes. You will know it has thickened to the right consistency when your spoon leaves a clean trail in the mixture when it is dragged along the bottom of the pan.

**3.** Transfer the hot flour mixture to a large bowl or stand mixer fitted with a dough hook attachment.

**4.** Add 2/3 cup cold milk straight out of the fridge, then add the remaining bread flour, the sugar, lemon zest, yeast, and salt.

**5.** Mix steadily to bring the dough together. I use a Danish dough whisk, or even a wooden spoon. Eventually as the dough gets thicker, I will just use my hands until the ingredients are all well-combined and begin to form a solid mass. If using a mixer, as soon as the dough begins to pull away from the sides of the bowl, stop mixing and knead by hand for about 15 minutes, until the dough is smooth, elastic, and tacky.

28 ounces Cherry Pie Filling
(see page 204 or used a
canned version)

**LEMON GLAZE**

3 cups powdered sugar

1 teaspoon lemon zest

¼ cup and 2 tablespoons
lemon juice

2 teaspoons vanilla extract

**6.** Shape the dough into a ball, place it in a lightly greased bowl, and cover.

**7.** Let the dough rise for 60 to 90 minutes, or until puffy. It's okay if it does not double in size.

**8.** If you're planning to make your own Cherry Pie Filling (see page 204), make it now while the dough is rising.

**9.** Line a baking sheet with parchment paper.

**10.** Transfer the dough to a lightly floured work surface and press it into a 10-by-12-inch rectangle that's about 1/2 inch thick.

**11.** Spread the cream cheese in a thin layer across the dough, covering all but a 1/2-inch strip along one long side.

**12.** Spread the Cherry Pie Filling across the cream cheese in an even layer.

**13.** Starting with the filling-covered long side, roll the dough gently but tightly.

**14.** Using a pastry cutter, sharp knife, or unflavored floss, cut the roll into 1 1/2- to 2-inch sections. Place the rolls onto the prepared baking sheet.

**15.** Cover the rolls with lightly greased plastic wrap and let them rise for 30 to 60 minutes. You will know they are done when the dough doesn't bounce back immediately if you press it with your finger.

**16.** Place a rack in the top third of your oven if possible, then preheat your oven to 375°F.

**17.** Bake the rolls until they're a light golden brown, 14 to 18 minutes.

LIGHT, FIRE, AND ABUNDANCE

**18.** Remove the rolls from the oven and top with the butter. Let cool for 10 to 15 minutes.

**19.** While the rolls cool, make the Lemon Icing: combine all the ingredients and stir together with a fork or whisk until smooth.

**20.** Once the rolls are fully cooled, dip a fork into your glaze and drizzle it across the tops or take a spoon and generously pour over. *There's no judgment here—make them unerringly delicious exactly how you want!*

evanescence

cherries

## CHERRY PIE FILLING

¼ cup cornstarch

¼ to ½ cup water

5 cups (about 2 pounds)
pitted cherries, fresh or
frozen

⅔ cup sugar, or more to
taste

1 tablespoon lemon
juice, or more to taste

1 tablespoon lemon zest

¾ teaspoon vanilla extract

¾ teaspoon cinnamon
powder

**1.** In a small bowl, mix together the cornstarch and 1/4 cup water if using frozen cherries or 1/2 cup water if using fresh cherries. This should create a slurry.

**2.** In a large pot, bring the cherries, sugar, lemon juice, and your cornstarch slurry to a boil over medium heat. Stir regularly as the sauce thickens, being careful not to break too many of the cherries.

**3.** When the cherries have softened and your spoon leaves a trail in the sauce, reduce the heat to low. I recommend setting a bit aside, letting it cool, and tasting to see if you need to sweeten it with more sugar or add more lemon juice to balance the sweetness that's developed. If you add either, make sure it is fully incorporated.

**4.** Remove the cherry mixture from the heat. Add the lemon zest, vanilla, and cinnamon.

**5.** Once cooled, use immediately for filling or store in an airtight container for up to 3 days. The mixture will thicken over time, so if you make this ahead of time, bring it to room temperature before using.

## S'MORES ROLLS

SERVES 10

S'mores are an absolute classic, stuffed with milk chocolate and memories of friends crowded 'round campfires, marshmallow noses, and sticky fingers under the stars.

### DOUGH

½ cup whole milk, room temperature, and ⅔ cup whole milk, cold

2 ½ cups and 3 tablespoons bread flour, and more for flouring the work surface

2 tablespoons sugar

2 tablespoons chocolate powder of choice (dark chocolate works well, but even hot chocolate mix or chocolate milk mix will work in a pinch!)

2 ½ teaspoons instant yeast

1 teaspoon salt

4 tablespoons unsalted butter, softened, and more for greasing the bowl and plastic wrap

*Ingredients continued on page 206*

**1.** Combine 1/2 cup room-temperature whole milk and 3 tablespoons bread flour in a small pot and stir until there are no lumps.

**2.** Place the pot over medium heat and cook, stirring regularly, for 1 to 3 minutes. You will know it has thickened to the right consistency when your spoon leaves a clean trail in the mixture when it is dragged along the bottom of the pan.

**3.** Transfer the hot flour mixture to a large bowl or stand mixer fitted with a dough hook attachment.

**4.** Add 2/3 cup cold milk straight out of the fridge, then add the remaining bread flour, the sugar, chocolate powder, yeast, and salt.

**5.** Mix steadily to bring the dough together. I use a Danish dough whisk, or even a wooden spoon. Eventually as the dough gets thicker, I will just use my hands until the ingredients are all well combined and begin to form a solid mass. If using the mixer, as soon as the dough begins to pull away from the sides of the bowl, stop mixing and knead the dough by hand for about 15 minutes, until it's smooth, elastic, and tacky.

**6.** Shape the dough into a ball, place it in a lightly greased bowl, and cover.

**7.** Let the dough rise for 60 to 90 minutes, or until

## FILLING

1 cup hazelnut spread (such
  as Nutella)

1 cup mini marshmallows

¼ cup crushed graham
  crackers

## S'MORES VANILLA
## GLAZE

1 cup powdered sugar

¼ teaspoon salt

2 tablespoons unsalted
  butter, melted

1 ½ tablespoons whole milk

1 tablespoon vanilla extract

puffy. It's okay if it does not double in size.

**8.** Line a baking sheet with parchment paper.

**9.** Transfer the dough to a lightly floured work surface and handpress it into a 10-by-12-inch rectangle that's about 1/2 inch thick.

**10.** Use a spatula or butter knife to spread the hazelnut spread across the dough covering all but a 1/2-inch strip along one long side.

**11.** Top the hazelnut spread with the marshmallows and graham cracker crumbs.

**12.** Starting with the filling-covered long side, roll the dough gently but tightly.

**13.** Using a pastry cutter, sharp knife, or unflavored floss, cut the roll into 1 1/2- to 2-inch sections. Place the rolls onto the prepared baking sheet.

**14.** Cover the rolls with lightly greased plastic wrap and let them rise for 30 to 60 minutes. You will know they are done when the dough doesn't bounce back immediately if you press it with your finger.

**15.** Place a rack in the top third of your oven if possible, then preheat your oven to 375°F.

**16.** Bake the rolls until they're a light golden brown, 14 to 18 minutes.

**17.** Remove the rolls from the oven and top with the butter. Let cool for 10 to 15 minutes.

**18.** To make the S'mores Vanilla Glaze, whisk all the ingredients together until they form a thick glaze (think the consistency of a glue).

**19.** Drizzle the room-temperature glaze over the cooled cinnamon rolls, giving it a fresh whisk before drizzling if necessary.

## PECAN PIE ROLLS

SERVES 10

These pecans will bring all kinds of success—likely including you being named the person who brought the best treats.

### DOUGH

½ cup whole milk, room temperature, and ⅔ cup whole milk, cold

2 ½ cups and 3 tablespoons bread flour, and more for flouring the work surface

2 tablespoons sugar

2 ½ teaspoons instant yeast

1 teaspoon salt

4 tablespoons unsalted butter, softened, and more for greasing the bowl and plastic wrap

*Ingredients continued on page 208*

*Ingredients continued on page 208*

**1.** Combine 1/2 cup room-temperature whole milk and 3 tablespoons bread flour in a small pot and stir until there are no lumps.

**2.** Place the pot over medium heat and cook, stirring regularly, for 1 to 3 minutes. You will know it has thickened to the right consistency when your spoon leaves a clean trail in the mixture when it is dragged along the bottom of the pan.

**3.** Transfer the hot flour mixture to a large bowl or stand mixer fitted with a dough hook attachment.

**4.** Add 2/3 cup cold milk straight out of the fridge, then add the remaining bread flour, the sugar, yeast, and salt.

**5.** Mix steadily to bring the dough together. I use a Danish dough whisk, or even a wooden spoon. Eventually as the dough gets thicker, I will just use my hands until the ingredients are all well combined and begin to form a solid mass. If using a mixer, as soon as the dough begins to pull away from the sides of the bowl, stop mixing and knead the dough by hand for about 15 minutes, until it's smooth, elastic, and tacky.

**6.** Shape the dough into a ball, place it in a lightly greased bowl, and cover.

## FILLING

¼ cup light corn syrup

1 egg

2 teaspoons vanilla extract

1 cup chopped pecans

½ packed cup dark brown
  sugar

1 tablespoon cinnamon
  powder

½ cup (1 stick) unsalted
  butter, softened

## MAPLE GLAZE

1 cup powdered sugar

3 tablespoons unsalted
  butter or margarine,
  softened

3 tablespoons (1 ½ ounces)
  cream cheese, softened

3 to 4 tablespoons maple
  syrup

**7.** Let the dough rise for 60 to 90 minutes, or until puffy. It's okay if it does not double in size.

**8.** While the dough is rising, make the filling: in a small bowl, whisk together the corn syrup, egg, and vanilla extract until combined. Add the pecans and mix. Set aside.

**9.** In a separate small bowl, mix together the brown sugar and cinnamon with a fork until combined. Set aside.

**10.** Line a baking sheet with parchment paper.

**11.** Transfer the dough to a lightly floured work surface and press it into a 10-by-12-inch rectangle that's about 1/2 inch thick.

**12.** Spread the softened butter for the filling over the dough, covering all but a 1/2-inch strip along one long side.

**13.** Sprinkle the brown sugar and cinnamon mix over the butter.

**14.** Using a spoon, add bits of the pecan mixture over the cinnamon sugar, distributing it evenly and pressing it lightly into the filling using a spoon or your fingers.

**15.** Starting with the filling-covered long side, roll the dough gently but tightly.

**16.** Using a pastry cutter, sharp knife, or unflavored floss, cut the roll into 1 1/2- to 2-inch sections. Place the rolls onto the prepared baking sheet.

**17.** Cover the rolls with lightly greased plastic wrap and let them rise for 30 to 60 minutes. You will know they are done when the dough doesn't bounce back immediately if you press it with your finger.

**18.** Place a rack in the top third of your oven if possible, then preheat your oven to 375°F.

**19.** Bake the rolls until they're a light golden brown, 14 to 18 minutes.

**20.** Remove the rolls from the oven and top with the butter. Let cool for 10 to 15 minutes.

**21.** While the rolls cool, make the Maple Glaze: in a large bowl, beat all the ingredients with an electric mixer on low speed, starting with 3 tablespoons of maple syrup. This should make a smooth, soft glaze that will drip nicely off a dipped fork or spoon. If you feel it's too thick, add the extra tablespoon of maple syrup.

**22.** Once the rolls are fully cooled, dip a fork into your glaze and drizzle it across the tops or take a spoon and generously pour over.

success

pecan

## ORANGE SPICE ROLLS

SERVES 10

I think of my brother-in-law Ben when I make these and his love of the chocolate-orange candies that come out every winter holiday season. These rolls are a delicious warm take on those cold-season chocolate confections, bringing forth warm memories of rambunctious gatherings and holding loved ones close in the magical spaces that happen between cold, snowy days and long, moon-filled nights.

### FILLING

1 ¼ packed cups light
    brown sugar

1 tablespoon cinnamon
    powder

½ teaspoon ground cloves

¼ teaspoon cardamom
    powder

¼ teaspoon salt

¼ teaspoon nutmeg
    powder

½ cup (1 stick) unsalted
    butter, room temperature

1 tablespoon clementine or
    orange zest

1 teaspoon lemon zest

*Ingredients continued on
    page 211*

**1.** Combine 1/2 cup room-temperature whole milk and 3 tablespoons bread flour in a small pot and stir until there are no lumps.

**2.** Place the pot over medium heat and cook, stirring regularly, for 1 to 3 minutes. You will know it has thickened to the right consistency when your spoon leaves a clean trail in the mixture when it is dragged along the bottom of the pan.

**3.** Transfer the hot flour mixture to a large bowl or stand mixer fitted with a dough hook attachment.

**4.** Add 2/3 cup cold milk straight out of the fridge, then add the remaining bread flour, the sugar, yeast, and salt.

**5.** Mix steadily to bring the dough together. I use a Danish dough whisk, or even a wooden spoon. Eventually as the dough gets thicker, I will just use my hands until the ingredients are all well combined and begin to form a solid mass. If using a mixer, as soon as the dough begins to pull away from the sides of the bowl, stop mixing and knead the dough by

**GLAZE**

1 cup powdered sugar

8 ounces cream cheese, room temperature

2 tablespoons freshly squeezed clementine or orange juice, or more as needed

1 tablespoon clementine or orange zest

hand for about 15 minutes, until it's smooth, elastic, and tacky.

**6.** Shape the dough into a ball, place it in a lightly greased bowl, and cover.

**7.** Let the dough rise for 60 to 90 minutes, or until puffy. It's okay if it does not double in size.

**8.** While the dough is rising, make the filling: in a small bowl, combine the brown sugar, cinnamon, cloves, cardamom, salt, and nutmeg. Set aside.

**9.** Line a baking sheet with parchment paper.

**10.** Transfer the dough to a lightly floured work surface and press it into a 10-by-12-inch rectangle that's about 1/2 inch thick.

**11.** Spread the butter for the filling across the dough, covering all but a 1/2-inch strip along one long side.

**12.** Sprinkle the brown sugar mixture across the butter. Spread the clementine and lemon zests on the sugar mixture.

**13.** Starting with the filling-covered long side, roll the dough gently but tightly.

**14.** Using a pastry cutter, sharp knife, or unflavored floss, cut the roll into 1-1/2 to 2-inch sections. Place the rolls onto the prepared baking sheet.

**15.** Cover the rolls with lightly greased plastic wrap and let them rise for 30 to 60 minutes. You will know they are done when the dough doesn't bounce back immediately if you press it with your finger.

**16.** Place a rack in the top third of your oven if possible, then preheat your oven to 375°F.

**17.** Bake the rolls until they're a light golden brown, 14 to 18 minutes.

**18.** Remove the rolls from the oven and top with the butter. Let cool for 10 to 15 minutes.

**19.** While the rolls cool, make the glaze: in a large bowl, beat all the ingredients with an electric mixer on low speed until smooth. This should make a smooth, soft glaze that will drip nicely off a dipped fork or spoon. If you feel it's too thick, add a bit of extra juice.

**20.** Once the rolls are fully cooled, dip a fork into your glaze and drizzle it across the tops or take a spoon and generously pour over.

# Banana Breads

## SAMAIRE AND DADDY'S GOLDEN BANANA BREAD

MAKES 8 SERVINGS

When my daughter was seven, she decided she wanted to learn how to make the perfect banana bread for her father. We spent weeks making it over and over again to get it right. Now, every spring, we pull out our recipe and bake that bread once again. As it's a recipe made by and for a child, the measurements are pretty loose.

Bringing intention to your dish doesn't always mean you need elaborate ingredients or complex steps. Sometimes the intention appears in the effort, excitement, and joy brought to the process of the making. The main goal with this recipe has always been to pour as much excitement about adventures yet to come, and love of the person you will share them with, into making it. If you do that, you're guaranteed amazing results.

5 tablespoons and 1 teaspoon unsalted butter

8 medium bananas: 6 overripe and 2 ripe

1 egg

¾ cup sugar

2 teaspoons vanilla extract

1 teaspoon baking soda

Pinch salt

1 ½ cups all-purpose flour

Butterscotch chips, to taste

½ packed cup brown sugar

Baking spray

**1.** Preheat your oven to 350°F.

**2.** Melt the butter in a small bowl. We usually microwave it for 20 to 30 seconds; it doesn't need to be completely melted.

**3.** Peel and slice the 6 overripe bananas. This is an excellent task for small hands, as the bananas don't require sharp knives and don't need to be perfectly, or even neatly, sliced.

**4.** Once the bananas are sliced, put them in a medium bowl and mash. The bananas should lose their shape, but remaining a little chunky in spots is good.

**5.** Pour in the butter and add the egg. Since I often have small people making this recipe with me, we

crack the egg into a separate small bowl and beat it with a fork before adding it to the banana and butter mixture to avoid any unwanted shell pieces making an appearance.

**6.** Stir until combined well. This can easily be done with a spoon or fork.

**7.** Once your mixture is combined, add the sugar and vanilla. Mix well, then add the baking soda and pinch of salt.

**8.** Add the flour about 1/2 cup at a time, slowly stirring to blend.

**9.** Sprinkle in the butterscotch chips to taste—I try to keep it to two child's handfuls—then add the brown sugar, which you can measure out, but it's also usually two little handfuls. Stir the chips and sugar into the batter.

**10.** Peel and thinly slice the 2 ripe bananas.

**11.** Spray a 4-by-8-inch loaf pan with baking spray to keep the batter from sticking. Pour the batter into the pan and top with the sliced ripe bananas. We like to make flower patterns with them along the top of the loaf.

**12.** Cook the bread for 1 hour. *Serve to someone you love dearly with a big smile on your face.*

OPPOSITE, TOP TO BOTTOM: SAMAIRE AND DADDY'S GOLDEN BANANA BREAD, CINNAMON BANANA BREAD (SEE PAGE 216), AND CLASSIC BANANA BREAD (SEE PAGE 218).

## CINNAMON BANANA BREAD

MAKES 8 SERVINGS

With swirls of warm, sweet cinnamon running through this bread, we are bound to remember that there is no perfect straight road. Our paths are winding and wandering, beautiful and daring, and through it all entwined in the warmth and love of those around us.

1 cup (2 sticks) and 6 to
  7 tablespoons unsalted
  butter, divided, and more
  for greasing the pan

2 eggs

2 tablespoons vanilla extract

2 cups all-purpose flour

1 ¼ cups sugar, divided

1 teaspoon baking soda

5 overripe bananas,
  mashed, and 6 thin slices
  of banana

¼ cup and 2 tablespoons
  dark brown sugar

¼ cup and 2 tablespoons
  cinnamon powder

**1.** Preheat your oven to 350°F.

**2.** Lightly grease a 5-by-9-inch loaf pan and then set it aside.

**3.** In a large bowl, melt 1 cup of the butter, then let it cool for 3 to 5 minutes.

**4.** Mix in the eggs, vanilla, flour, 1 cup of the sugar, and the baking soda.

**5.** Fold in the mashed bananas until just combined.

**6.** In a separate small bowl, melt 6 tablespoons butter. Then use a fork to stir in the remaining 1/4 cup sugar and the brown sugar and cinnamon, stirring until well combined. The mixture should be thick but still able to swirl into the dough. If you feel it's too thick, add another tablespoon of melted butter.

**7.** Spread one-quarter of the batter evenly into the bottom of the prepared pan.

**8.** Dollop one-quarter of the cinnamon-sugar mixture over the batter in the pan. Using a knife or the handle of a wooden spoon, swirl the sugar through the batter. Repeat two more times.

**9.** Spread the remaining batter along the top of the loaf and sprinkle with the remaining cinnamon sugar. Dip a knife or spoon handle into the entire loaf and make large swirls.

**10.** Place the thin banana slices down the middle of the batter.

**11.** Place the loaf pan on a baking sheet and bake for about 1 hour, or until a toothpick placed in the center of the loaf comes out clean.

**12.** Let the bread cool in the pan for at least 30 minutes, then remove to cool on a wire rack.

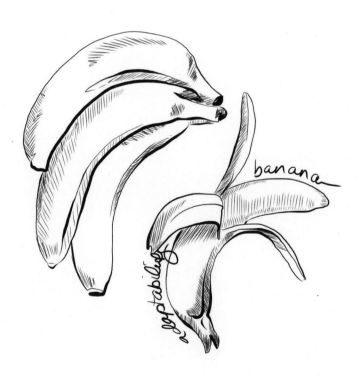

## CLASSIC BANANA BREAD

MAKES 16 SERVINGS

Simple and beloved, the banana is a popular fruit. (It's actually a *berry*! Can you believe it? No? Look it up and be, as I was, *amazed*.) This bread? Also simple and beloved. Bananas are said to grant resilience during change, enabling us to pivot when our situation or the world around us shifts in some way—like when we learn that bananas are berries.

5 tablespoons and 1 teaspoon unsalted butter, softened, and more for greasing the pans

1 ¼ cups sugar

2 eggs

5 large overripe bananas, mashed

¾ cup sour cream

1 teaspoon vanilla extract

2 ½ cups all-purpose flour

2 teaspoons baking soda

1 teaspoon cinnamon powder

½ teaspoon nutmeg powder

½ teaspoon salt

**1.** Preheat your oven to 325°F and generously grease two 4-by-8-inch loaf pans.

**2.** Cream the butter and sugar in a large bowl using an electric mixer, sturdy spoon, or dough whisk.

**3.** Add the eggs and mix until well combined.

**4.** Stir in the bananas, sour cream, and vanilla.

**5.** In a separate bowl, mix together the flour, baking soda, cinnamon, nutmeg, and salt.

**6.** Mix the flour mixture into the wet ingredients until the flour is fully combined.

**7.** Divide the batter evenly between the two loaf pans.

**8.** Bake for 1 hour or until a toothpick inserted into the center of each loaf comes out clean.

**9.** Let cool, then remove from the pan. Enjoy!

# Pumpkin Muffins MAKES 24 MUFFINS

This simple, quick recipe is perfect for a yum-tastic fall treat and wards against spitefulness, though I don't know who's going to be spiteful if you hand them one of these muffins.

Baking spray

15 ounces boxed spice cake mix, or vanilla cake mix, if you can't find spice

15 ounces canned pumpkin purée

6 ounces chocolate chips (optional)

**1.** Preheat your oven to 325°F. Prep a 12-cup muffin pan with paper or silicone cups and a light coating of baking spray. If you have two pans and an oven that fits two pans, you can prep them both here. (In my microscopic kitchen in Hell's Kitchen, New York, I bake these in batches.)

**2.** In a medium bowl, stir together the cake mix and pumpkin purée.

**3.** If adding chocolate chips, fold them into the batter.

**4.** Scoop the batter into the muffin cups, filling each about three-quarters full.

**5.** Bake for 18 to 20 minutes, or until a toothpick comes out clean.

**6.** Let cool for about 10 minutes (until cool enough to touch), then remove from pan and allow to finish cooling on a rack.

*Sweetness and light*

# DESSERT

**FROM A SMALL BITE** of something sweet to elaborate concoctions made for a crowd, there's something that feels extra special about being given, or giving, a small sweetness. Intrinsically tied to love and care, the creation of a confection is a universal act of tenderness. Making one can transport us to the moments before a joyful gathering, standing among those we love most, stirring up batters, stories, and laughter. Eating these decadent dishes transports us just as easily, bringing back holidays, celebrations, even the simple moments carved into our hearts in chocolate, cream, and delight.

Never doubt the power of a gift, freely given, of consideration and time. It is no small thing and has no small impact. Our world could use more moments filled with sweetness and light. The treasure may be small, but the intention and effect are immeasurable.

# Orange Fluff SERVES 10

Oranges bring joy, there's no denying it. Small, bright bits of sunshine that appear in the depths of winter, advising us that there is light to be found if we seek it out. This dessert never fails to make me happy.

3 ounces boxed orange-
  flavored instant gelatin mix
  (like Jell-O)

1 cup boiling water

½ cup cold water

3 ounces boxed instant
  vanilla pudding powder

8 ounces whipped topping,
  thawed

14 ounces canned
  mandarin oranges, drained

10 ounces mini
  marshmallows

**1.** In a small saucepan, combine the boiling water and the orange gelatin mix. Whisk until the gelatin mix is fully dissolved.

**2.** Pour the mixture into a large bowl and add the cold water.

**3.** Place the bowl in the refrigerator and allow to chill for 15 minutes.

**4.** Remove the bowl from the refrigerator and slowly whisk in the vanilla pudding powder until smooth.

**5.** Chill in the refrigerator for another 15 to 20 minutes, or until slightly thickened.

**6.** Fold in the whipped topping, mandarin oranges, and marshmallows.

**7.** Chill again for at least 1 hour before serving.

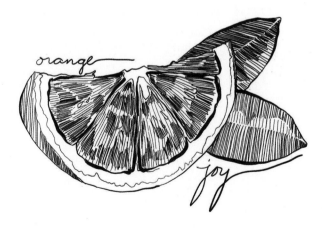

orange

joy

# Strawberry Cream Cake SERVES 8 TO 10

Strawberries and cream is one of my favorite flavor combinations. Strawberries are said to be the food of the fairies, magical and enticing. It's not hard to see why, because while this may seem like a summertime treat, it's also perfect in the darkness of winter when you are ready to conjure up a sweet, bright day. You won't be disappointed.

13 ounces boxed angel
  food cake mix
3 ounces boxed strawberry-
  flavored instant gelatin mix
  (like Jell-O)
1 ¼ cups boiling water
1 pound frozen strawberries
8 ounces whipped topping,
  thawed

**1.** Bake the angel food cake according to its directions and let cool. *I always use a store-bought mix because I have a tendency not to plan ahead well with this recipe. Angel food cake is super easy to make, but sometimes I just want something quick to put together that still feels special, and this fits the bill. All the better that I need not dirty extra dishes.*

**2.** Tear or cut the angel food cake into slightly larger-than-bite-size pieces (1 to 2 inches). Set aside.

**3.** Combine the gelatin mix and boiling water in a saucepan or heatproof bowl. Whisk until the gelatin mix is fully dissolved.

**4.** Add the frozen strawberries to the gelatin and stir carefully to coat them completely.

**5.** Transfer the coated strawberries to a large bowl and let cool in the refrigerator for about 5 minutes.

**6.** Fold the whipped topping into the strawberry-gelatin mixture.

**7.** Gently fold the angel food cake pieces into the strawberry mixture.

**8.** Pour the mixture into a 7-by-11-inch or similar-size pan.

**9.** Place the pan in the refrigerator and just chill for 2 to 3 hours. You and the cake both. *No, seriously. Place that pan into the refrigerator and go read a wonderful book or watch that movie you've been dying to see. Draw something. Take a walk. Enjoy the next 2 to 3 hours (or longer—it won't do it any harm) as it comes together. This gives you some time to come together too.*

**10.** Celebrate with a creamy slice of Strawberry Cream Cake.

# Dark-Side Monster Cake Cookies

MAKES 24 COOKIES

These cookies are one of Wylie's favorite treats. I originally made them for his fourth birthday, and I still remember how excited he was to have "dark-side cookies" to go with his *Star Wars* theme. The cookies are dark and decadent, and perfect with a glass of cold milk. They can be filled with any chips or small chocolate candy of your choice. Experiment and create your own delicious combination.

15 ounces boxed chocolate
  cake mix

½ packed cup brown sugar

¾ cup (1 ½ sticks) unsalted
  butter, softened

½ cup peanut butter

1 egg, beaten

2 tablespoons milk

1 tablespoon and 1
  teaspoon vanilla extract

2 cups oats

½ cup M&M's

½ cup peanut butter chips
  or your favorite candy chip

**1.** Preheat your oven to 350°F. Line a baking sheet with parchment paper or a silicone baking mat and set aside.

**2.** In a stand mixer fitted with a paddle attachment, mix together the cake mix, brown sugar, butter, peanut butter, egg, milk, and vanilla on medium speed until fully combined. If, like me, you have no space for a stand mixer, feel free to use a large bowl and a wooden spoon or Danish dough whisk—and congratulate yourself on building some serious muscle!

**3.** Use a wooden spoon to fold in the oats, M&M's, and peanut butter chips until just combined. Reserve a few M&M's to put on top of the cookies.

**4.** Use a cookie scoop—or tablespoon, or any scoop of your choice—to drop balls of dough (about the size of a large gumball or Gobstopper, or slightly smaller than a golf ball—hey, we all have our relevant frames of reference) 2 inches apart on the prepared baking sheet.

**5.** Add a few M&M's to the top of each cookie dough ball, gently pressing them into the dough.

**6.** Bake for 12 to 15 minutes, or until the tops of the cookies are set.

**7.** Cool for 5 minutes on the baking sheet before transferring to a cooling rack to cool completely.

# Red Velvet Cookies MAKES 20 COOKIES

While the Dark-Side Monster Cake Cookies (see page 225) are Wylie's favorite, these are Samaire's preferred cookie, hands down. They are wonderful for Valentine's Day, winter holidays, or any day you want a rich, ruby-colored dessert.

15 ounces boxed red velvet
  cake mix
⅓ cup vegetable oil
2 eggs, room temperature
1 cup white chocolate chips

**1.** Preheat your oven to 350°F. Line a baking sheet with parchment paper or a silicone baking mat and set aside.

**2.** Using a large bowl and a wooden spoon or a stand mixer fitted with a paddle attachment, mix together the cake mix, oil, and eggs on medium speed until fully combined.

**3.** Add the white chocolate chips and use a wooden spoon to fold them into the dough until well combined.

**4.** Scoop 2-tablespoon-size balls of cookie dough onto the prepared baking sheet, making sure to leave a little room between each cookie.

**5.** Bake for 10 to 12 minutes, until the tops of the cookies are set.

**6.** Remove the cookies from the oven and allow them to cool for 5 to 10 minutes on the baking sheet before transferring them to a wire rack to finish cooling.

# Rainbow Cookies MAKES 20 COOKIES

These are cookies I have tried to perfect over the years simply because my husband, Sam, loves them so much. I adore them not just for the smile they bring to his face, a smile filled with memories of childhood holidays, but for their joyful presence on any plate or within any care package. Whether you have had them before or are just discovering them, they can't help but brighten your day.

½ cup (1 stick) unsalted
  butter, softened, and more
  for greasing the pan
½ cup sugar
1 egg
1 ½ cups all-purpose flour
¼ teaspoon baking powder
¼ teaspoon baking soda
4 (3-ounce) packages
  instant gelatin mix (like
  Jell-O; choose four
  different flavors that align
  with your favorite colors)

**1.** Preheat your oven to 350°F. Lightly grease a baking sheet.

**2.** In a medium bowl, cream the butter and sugar with an electric mixer, sturdy wooden spoon, or dough whisk.

**3.** Add the egg and mix to combine.

**4.** In a separate bowl, combine the flour, baking powder, and baking soda.

**5.** Add the flour mixture to the bowl with the butter, sugar, and egg. Mix until no signs of the flour remain.

**6.** Divide the dough equally into four separate bowls.

**7.** Place 1/4 cup of gelatin powder into each bowl, using a different flavor for each bowl. Knead the dough in each bowl until the ingredients are fully combined and the color is consistent.

**8.** Using a cookie scoop or tablespoon, scoop balls of dough approximately 2 inches in diameter (don't fret the exactitude) from each bowl and place them on the prepared baking sheet. Flatten each gently into a round with the back of a spoon.

**9.** Bake the cookies for 10 minutes, until the edges just begin to brown. *There is much debate in our family* *as to the perfect Rainbow Cookie baking time—one contin-gent insists on these being just slightly underdone, so they are soft, baked for about 8 minutes. Another insists that they be browned, having been baked for approximately 12 minutes. I have, here, split the difference. Pick your side, or go for the middle road.*

**10.** Once the cookies have baked to your liking, remove them from the oven and let them sit on the baking sheet for 5 minutes before transferring to a cooling rack.

**11.** Pick your favorite color and enjoy!

# Peanut Butter Cookies MAKES 6 COOKIES

We all have certain recipes we keep close because they came from someone we held dear who has long since passed. These are recipes that we make as a meditation, a ritual, a comfort—an act that brings our loved ones back in a small way, if only for a short while.

And sometimes, that's how we introduce those we love currently to those who came before. Grandma's recipe may not let your friends and family hear her laugh, but it will let them relive a moment you treasure in a place beyond time. That is how this recipe came to me, through my dearest friend, Leslie. Her grandmother Waneta used to make these cookies with her. Waneta is no stranger to me; I know her well through the stories Leslie has told me over the years. And now I can make these cookies with my kids, as Les made them with her grandma, retelling the stories I know and passing along her wisdom that has been passed to me. Sometimes the best recipes are ones that build a bridge between a moment long past and the one we find ourselves standing in today. They offer a way to extend a magical moment—one that, while all too brief in reality, becomes timeless in practice and, even more magically, becomes one we can share across time and generations.

And so as we roll out the dough I say to my children, echoing Leslie's voice to her children, as Waneta's to her own, "We are people of hope." Then I count our blessings and name our gratitude with each turn of the spoon in the bowl. All for simple peanut butter cookies that offer so very much more. This is magic in the kitchen.

1 cup peanut butter

1 cup white sugar

1 egg

**1.** Preheat your oven to 350°F.

**2.** Mix all the ingredients together in a bowl using an electric mixer or a wooden spoon until smooth and creamy.

**3.** Using a tablespoon, scoop the batter out of the bowl and roll it in your palms to form small balls.

**4.** Place the balls of dough on a parchment-paper-lined baking sheet with a couple inches between each one. Press a fork into each, making a crisscross pattern.

**5.** Bake for 10 minutes.

**6.** Cool the cookies on the baking sheet for 2 minutes before moving to a cooling rack or plate.

# Chocolate Pudding Cake SERVES 8

In the midst of creams and bright berries and all that comes with celebrating the bright days that pass, I like to sometimes make a little something to remind us of the darker nights worth recognizing too. The darkness that appears in our lives is not always that of doom and gloom; it can arrive as a signal for rest, an opportunity to slow down and plan, or a simple time to rejuvenate and reset. When this inevitably happens, whether it be in our own existing rhythms or as the light of the sun slowly relinquishes to the moon in the back half of the year, it's worth relishing. We don't often give ourselves time to simply be, to slow down and rest, or even just stop and plan. This cake celebrates all that rich darkness can give us. It is a special kind of decadence and delineation from our rush of days, a celebration of, and reason to give, space to breathe.

1 cup all-purpose flour

¾ cup sugar

⅓ cup and 2 tablespoons cocoa powder, divided

2 tablespoons baking powder

¼ teaspoon salt

½ cup milk

2 tablespoons unsalted butter, melted

1 packed cup brown sugar

1 ⅓ cups hot water

Whipped cream for garnishing (optional)

Berries for garnishing (optional)

**1.** Preheat your oven to 350°F.

**2.** In a large mixing bowl, combine the flour, sugar, 2 tablespoons cocoa powder, baking powder, and salt.

**3.** Slowly stir in the milk and butter.

**4.** Pour the batter into a square 9-by-9-inch baking pan.

**5.** In a small bowl, stir together the brown sugar and remaining 1/3 cup cocoa powder until well combined.

**6.** Sprinkle the brown sugar mixture over the cake batter.

**7.** Pour the hot water over everything in your pan.

**8.** Carefully place the pan in the oven and bake for 45 minutes.

**9.** Invert onto a dessert plate, cut the cake into squares, and serve hot.

**10.** Make sure to spoon any extra pudding over the cake and top with whipped cream and berries. *You can also wait for it to cool and serve it cold; I am just never quite able to make it that far. Once, when I was pregnant with Samaire, I made this cake for Midsummer and ended up eating the whole pan myself with a spoon, straight out of the baking dish—not my proudest moment, but it was delicious nonetheless.*

# Ooey Gooey Butter Cake SERVES 12

This cake, for me, is the perfect example of the transportive power of a simple dish. There's not much that goes into making an Ooey Gooey Butter Cake, yet whenever I have this cake I can't help but hear the strains of Tom Petty and the Heartbreakers playing "Wildflowers" and see the smile of one of my very dearest friends.

The first time I had this cake, my friend Scott bought me one for my birthday from a bakery in St. Louis, Missouri, while I was visiting him there. I was feeling a bit unmoored and unsure and had sought out the company of one of my best friends. We were both in college and funds were scarce, but he had gone to a special bakery to buy me this cake, as he knew I'd love to celebrate my day. I remember feeling so unbelievably loved in the moment he opened up the box.

Sugar is often used to sweeten hearts and is an ingredient in love spells, but sometimes, like with *my* Ooey Gooey Butter Cake, it's a way to reveal a sweet heart, one that cares, one that holds steadfast to a friendship meant to last the ages. Scott gave me that cake more than twenty years ago, and today we have been friends for more than thirty years. This cake will never not remind me of him and the delicious sweetness of the people who stay with us as we grow to be who we are meant to be.

## CAKE (THE OOEY)

16 ½ ounces boxed yellow cake mix

½ cup (1 stick) unsalted butter, melted, and more for greasing the pan

1 egg

*Ingredients continued on page 238*

*Ingredients continued on page 238*

**1.** Preheat your oven to 350°F and lightly grease a 9-by-13-inch baking pan.

**2.** To make the cake, mix together the cake mix, butter, and egg in a medium bowl until well combined.

**3.** Pat the mixture into the bottom of the prepared baking pan. Without much moisture, the batter should form a crust-like layer along the bottom of the pan. This may feel a bit weird, but I promise it works! It works so deliciously.

## TOPPING
## (THE GOOEY)

8 ounces cream cheese,
softened

½ cup (1 stick) unsalted
butter, melted

2 eggs

1 tablespoon and 1
teaspoon vanilla extract

16 ounces (2 cups)
powdered sugar

**4.** In a separate bowl, combine the cream cheese, butter, eggs, and vanilla for the topping and stir vigorously or beat with an electric mixer until smooth.

**5.** Add the powdered sugar and mix well. *I inevitably make a giant mess in this moment because I'm so impatient, so here's a great place to take a deep breath, slow down, and enjoy the process. Drop the powdered sugar in a little at a time, remembering how the sweetest moments seem to always go by all too fast. Resolve that the ones ahead will happen at a more even pace. Promise yourself to enjoy one moment at a time, each as it happens, as every small scoop of sugar joins the batter.*

**6.** Spread the topping evenly over the cake batter crust.

**7.** Bake 40 to 50 minutes. The center should still be gooey when you remove the cake.

**8.** Serve warm. *No need to be exceedingly patient with this joyful moment.*

# Ooey Gooey Pumpkin Cake SERVES 12

This is a wonderful cake to make in the fall. In my family we make it for Samhain, the last of the harvest festivals, which falls in the calendar near Halloween. On Samhain we embrace pumpkin as a summoner, a perfect tool for a night where we honor and tell the tales of those we love who have left this world. This pumpkin cake works easily as well for Halloween, as it's a symbol of prosperity and ideal for a night filled with an abundance of sweets and treats.

One Halloween night there was an accident involving an immersion blender while making this cake and a subsequent trip to the ER (during which my friend Mikki told the taxi driver I had given birth to two kids sans drugs, so "not to worry, we are fine," as he struggled to find the right entrance to the hospital). After we finally got settled, we drove a nurse nuts with our jokes and iPhone documentary plans. Thankfully, everyone got through fairly unscathed. It's now the "story never to be told" at our house, but here I am telling you, because we never did make our documentary (silly no-filming-allowed rules at the hospital), and it feels worth documenting in some way, despite the fact that I'm sparing you the goriest, most Halloween-ific details.

## CAKE
## (THE OOEY)

16 ½ ounces boxed yellow
  cake mix (boxed)

½ cup (1 stick) unsalted
  butter, melted, and more
  for greasing the pan

1 egg

*Ingredients continued on*

*page 240*

**1.** Preheat your oven to 350°F and lightly grease a 9-by-13-inch baking pan.

**2.** For the cake, mix together the cake mix, butter, and egg in a medium bowl until well combined.

**3.** Pat the mixture into the bottom of the prepared pan. Without much moisture, the batter should form a crust-like layer along the bottom of the pan.

**4.** To prepare the topping, combine the pumpkin and cream cheese in a large bowl and beat with an electric mixer or stir vigorously until smooth.

**5.** Add the eggs, butter, and vanilla, mixing until fully combined.

## TOPPING
## (THE GOOEY)

15 ounces canned pumpkin

8 ounces cream cheese, softened

3 eggs

½ cup (1 stick) unsalted butter, melted

2 teaspoons vanilla extract

16 ounces (2 cups) powdered sugar

1 teaspoon cinnamon powder

1 teaspoon nutmeg powder

Freshly whipped cream for serving (optional)

Cinnamon ice cream for serving (optional)

**6.** Add the powdered sugar, cinnamon, and nutmeg and stir until smooth and no trace of the white sugar remains.

**7.** Spread the topping over the cake batter.

**8.** Bake for 40 to 50 minutes. The cake's center should still be gooey when it is removed from the oven.

**9.** Serve warm topped with freshly whipped cream or with a side of cinnamon ice cream.

# Fairy Berries SERVES 1 SMALL MAGICAL CREATURE

Magic is often at its best when you're small, when holidays are filled with mythical guardians and small-winged creatures leave you gifts under your pillow in exchange for a baby tooth. I remember fondly how my daughter, Samaire, loved all stories of magical creatures, mythical folk, and superheroes when she was little.

I admit I did what I could to encourage it. We often lose our wonder in the world much too fast and spend years working to regain it. I wanted to stoke the fire of imagination and astonishment for as long as I could. And so we would wake up early, grab the Raggedy Ann and Andy bowl I'd had since I was small, and pick the best of the strawberries we had. We'd chop them up and then, with sticky, pink-stained fingers, we'd sprinkle fairy dust all across the top of them.

This recipe has been prepared for my magical creature, my little superhero, and my mythical fairy folk innumerable times. And now it is here for yours.

1 cup chopped strawberries

1 teaspoon sugar
(granulated or any other
sugar will do)

**1.** Place the strawberries into your favorite bowl.

**2.** Lightly sprinkle sugar over the strawberries, covering thoroughly.

**3.** Tell magical tales and list all the wonderful things that await you that day.

## Tip

Make sure to leave a strawberry or two outside your door for the fairies. They get very cross when you indulge without sharing.

# Ho Ho Cake MAKES 18 SERVINGS

Newlin, this recipe appears here because you asked if it would. This cake, which I made for your birthday so many years ago, was the first cake I ever made for anyone's birthday. It was the richest, most indulgent cake I could find to make, and it still is.

The cake gets its name from the delicious treat I found at gas stations growing up. It was a road trip staple, and this cake takes those rolled delights and unrolls them in a most yum-tastic way. All the delicious flavor of the childhood treat, but fresher and somehow more chocolatey. Magic is real.

Chocolate is love in all its forms, and this cake will deliver that in spades. It's perfect to give as a gift: a little different, a little extraordinary, a lot manageable to create. Make it for a friend who deserves to know how different, extraordinary, and not so manageable they are to you, for people who hold a special quirky and beloved place in your heart, just like my friend Newlin.

## CAKE

Baking spray

3 cups all-purpose flour

¼ cup and 2 tablespoons cocoa powder

1 ½ teaspoons baking soda

1 teaspoon salt

2 cups sugar

2 cups water

½ cup and 2 tablespoons vegetable oil

2 tablespoons vinegar

2 teaspoons vanilla extract

*Ingredients continued on*

*page 243*

**1.** Preheat your oven to 350°F and spray a 9-by-13-inch baking pan with baking spray.

**2.** For the cake, in a large bowl, whisk together the flour, cocoa powder, baking soda, and salt.

**3.** Add the sugar, water, vegetable oil, vinegar, and vanilla. Stir until well combined, then pour the mixture into your prepared baking pan.

**4.** Bake for 25 to 30 minutes, or until a toothpick or knife inserted comes out clean. Let cool completely, so the cream doesn't melt when you apply it.

**5.** While the cake cools, start the cream filling by whisking together the milk and flour in a saucepan.

**6.** Simmer over low heat until it thickens, 3 to 5 minutes. Set aside to cool.

## CREAM

1 cup milk, cold

¼ cup all-purpose flour

1 cup sugar

1 cup (2 sticks) unsalted
butter, softened

1 teaspoon vanilla extract

## CHOCOLATE TOPPING

3 cups powdered sugar

¼ cup and 2 tablespoons
cocoa powder

½ cup (1 stick) and 2
tablespoons unsalted
butter, melted

1 egg

2 ½ tablespoons hot water

1 teaspoon vanilla extract

**7.** Once the flour-and-milk mixture is cool, use an electric mixer, sturdy spoon, or dough whisk to cream together the sugar, butter, and vanilla until smooth and fluffy. *Sometimes it feels like maybe it won't come together, but have patience! It will happen, I promise. Just keep at it.*

**8.** Spread the cream onto the cooled cake.

**9.** For the chocolate topping, beat together all the ingredients with an electric mixer, sturdy spoon, or dough whisk until well combined. Look for a smooth, even color.

**10.** Pour or spoon the chocolate topping over the middle of the cake and smooth it to the cake's edges.

**11.** Chill for at least 30 minutes before serving.

# Elderberry Honey Cream Pie SERVES 8

The tartness of the elderberry jam in this pie pairs wonderfully with the sweet succulence of the honey—a dichotomy of flavors that brings both blessings and love to those who consume it. I've provided instructions here for making a homemade pie crust, but if you'd rather not, store-bought is fine too!

## CRUST

1 ¼ cups all-purpose flour, and more for flouring the work surface

¼ tablespoon sugar

¼ teaspoon sea salt

½ cup (1 stick) unsalted butter, cold, diced into ¼-inch pieces

½ cup ice water, and more as needed

*Ingredients continued on page 245*

## CRUST

**1.** Combine the flour, sugar, and salt in a food processor and pulse a few times, or mix with a whisk to combine.

**2.** Add the butter and pulse the mixture or use a pastry cutter to mix it in until coarse crumbs form with some pea-size pieces. The mixture should remain dry and powdery.

**3.** Add 1/2 cup ice water and continue to pulse or use the pastry cutter just until moist clumps or small balls form.

**4.** Press a piece of dough between your fingertips, and if the dough sticks together, you have added enough water. If it doesn't, add more water 1 teaspoon at a time. Be careful not to add too much water or the dough will be sticky and difficult to roll out.

**5.** Gather the dough into a ball in your hands. Don't knead the dough; just gather it and squeeze it together gently.

**6.** Transfer the dough to a clean work surface and flatten it to form a flat disk.

**7.** Cover the dough disk with plastic wrap and refrigerate it for 1 hour. When ready to use, remove

## PIE FILLING

½ cup elderberry preserves

2 cups milk

1 cup heavy cream

3 eggs

½ cup pure honey

⅓ packed cup light brown
  sugar

⅓ cup sugar

3 tablespoons cornstarch

1 teaspoon vanilla extract

⅛ teaspoon salt

## WHIPPED CREAM

1 cup heavy whipping
  cream

½ cup powdered sugar

1 tablespoon elderberry
  syrup

1 teaspoon vanilla extract

## FOR SERVING

Drizzle of honey (optional)

it from the refrigerator and let it come to room
temperature.

**8.** Preheat your oven to 350°F.

**9.** On a lightly floured surface, roll the crust to fit a
9-inch pie dish. Place the crust in the pie dish and
trim off any excess dough along the edges. Flute the
edges with your fingertips.

**10.** Gently press a fork's tines across the bottom of
the crust to create small pinpricks in the dough, then
place parchment over the dough and fill with pie
weights or dried beans. The holes in the crust allow
steam to escape the dough as it cooks, keeping it from
puffing up. The pie weights will ensure the pie has a
nice flat bottom.

**11.** Bake for 20 minutes, then remove the weights
and parchment paper, bake for another 8 minutes,
and remove the crust from the oven.

### FILLING

**1.** Raise the oven temperature to 375°F.

**2.** Spread the elderberry preserves evenly over
your crust.

**3.** In a pot set over medium-low heat, warm the milk
and cream until steaming.

**4.** Whisk the eggs, honey, sugars, cornstarch, vanilla,
and salt together in a medium bowl.

**5.** Slowly, so very slowly, drizzle the warm milk and
cream mixture into the egg mixture while whisking
continuously. This is important, as you don't want to
scramble your eggs, so keep the mixture moving!

**6.** Return the mixture to the original pot and cook over medium-low heat, stirring constantly with a wooden spoon, for 8 minutes, or until the custard thickens and begins to stick to the spoon.

**7.** Pour the thickened custard through a fine-mesh sieve into a bowl to locate and discard any small pieces of egg that may have scrambled. This will ensure you get a smooth custard. Pour the now-perfect custard into the pie crust.

**8.** Bake for 12 to 15 minutes, until the edges are set but the center remains a bit jiggly.

**9.** Let cool to room temperature, then place in the refrigerator for about 2 hours. Once the pie has cooled, it can be stored in the refrigerator for up to 1 week.

## WHIPPED CREAM

**1.** Using a whisk, hand mixer, or a stand mixer fitted with a whisk attachment, whip the heavy cream, powdered sugar, elderberry syrup, and vanilla until peaks form, 2 to 5 minutes. Do not over-whip or it will clump; you want to keep it smooth.

**2.** Either cover and place in the refrigerator to set or use immediately.

## FOR SERVING

**1.** When ready to serve, slice the pie and place each slice on a serving plate.

**2.** Top each piece with elderberry whipped cream and a drizzle of honey, if desired.

# Key Lime Pie SERVES 8

I'm not sure any one thing could taste of salty waves and dramatic sunsets more than this Key Lime Pie. The limes bring purification and luck, making this pie a sunny way to welcome a new turn: a job, a hobby, a vacation, or even just a nice start to the week.

I want to be up front and honest with you about this recipe: I don't make a crust or the whipped topping. Ever. Like, never ever. However, I have included it here if you'd like to. I'm just too lazy to be bothered when I can buy a premade crust and some whip of the Cool or Reddi variety. But I do stand by this complete version of the recipe; I have made it and it's delicious. I tested it just for you.

Odds are, though, if you ever eat a pie I made, you can thank Pillsbury for the crust. Why is this where I draw the line when I adore from-scratch pizza and empanada crusts? I just don't know. I wish I could tell you. Nonetheless, let's get down to business!

## GRAHAM CRACKER CRUST

1 ½ cups graham cracker crumbs

⅓ cup sugar

6 tablespoons unsalted butter, melted

*Ingredients continued on page 248*

## GRAHAM CRACKER CRUST

**1.** Preheat your oven to 375°F.

**2.** Mix the graham cracker crumbs, sugar, and butter in a medium bowl.

**3.** Press the crumb mixture in an even layer across the bottom and up the sides of an 8- to 9 1/2-inch round pie pan.

**4.** Bake for 7 minutes. Set aside and let cool for at least 30 minutes.

## PIE FILLING

**1.** Reduce the oven temperature to 350°F.

**2.** In a large bowl, beat the egg yolks with a mixer on medium speed or heartily by hand with a whisk until they thicken.

### PIE FILLING

4 egg yolks

14 ounces canned
   sweetened condensed
   milk

½ cup freshly squeezed
   key lime juice (juice of
   approximately 20 key
   limes)

1 tablespoon and 1
   teaspoon lime zest

### WHIPPED CREAM

1 cup heavy whipping
   cream

½ cup powdered sugar

1 teaspoon vanilla extract

### FOR SERVING

1 tablespoon and 1
   teaspoon lime zest

2 key limes, thinly sliced

**3.** Add the sweetened condensed milk, then turn the mixer speed to low.

**4.** Pour in half the lime juice.

**5.** Once the lime juice is fully incorporated, add the other half of the juice and the zest and continue mixing for another 10 to 20 seconds, until well combined.

**6.** Pour the filling into the cooled crust and bake for 12 minutes to set the yolks.

**7.** Remove the pie from the oven and cool to room temperature.

**8.** Once cooled, refrigerate for at least 2 hours. This can be stored in the refrigerator for up to 1 week.

### WHIPPED CREAM AND SERVING

**1.** Right before you serve the pie, beat the heavy whipping cream and powdered sugar together with a mixer until stiff peaks form, then beat in the vanilla.

**2.** Garnish the pie with additional lime zest, the whipped topping, and thin slices of key lime.

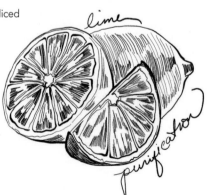

lime

purification

# Hot Chocolate Yule Cake SERVES 8

This is one of my very favorite cakes to make and it is always a hit, especially around the holidays. It's so fun to make an actual yule log cake, sprinkle it with sugar snow, and eat it under the twinkling lights of our way-too-big-for-our-apartment safety hazard of a tree.

But as much as we love this cake now, it took a while to get here. These rolled cakes terrified me. I tried to make a couple when the kids were really small, and they always seemed to crack and refuse to roll. After numerous attempts over the years, I hold fast to this recipe. It works almost every time, and while it's not always perfect, it's always dramatic and delicious. And even when it turns out a bit wonky, the frosting covers all the sins, so it's a perfect recipe to start with when trying to make a jelly roll cake—or a roulade, if you want to get fancy. I usually do.

I recommend buying a tub of chocolate frosting for this recipe; no matter what you do or do not celebrate, there's enough for you to do this time of year without making this from scratch.

## FILLING

1 ⅓ cups powdered sugar

¾ cup instant hot chocolate
mix (or four 1.38-ounce
envelopes)

1 teaspoon cinnamon
powder

2 cups heavy cream

*Ingredients continued on*
*page 251*

## FILLING

**1.** Beat the powdered sugar, hot chocolate mix, cinnamon, and heavy cream with a mixer on high speed until smooth with medium peaks.

**2.** Place the mixture in the refrigerator to set for at least 2 hours. You can make this up to a day ahead if desired.

## CAKE

**1.** Adjust your oven's rack to a middle position and then preheat the oven to 350°F.

**2.** Lightly grease a 13-by-18-inch rimmed baking sheet, line it with parchment paper, and lightly grease the parchment. It feels repetitive but will

## CAKE

Butter or oil for greasing
  the pan

1 ⅓ cups cake flour

¾ cup sugar

1 ½ teaspoons baking
  powder

¼ teaspoon salt

¾ cup instant hot chocolate
  mix (or four 1.38-ounce
  envelopes)

⅓ cup water

5 eggs, yolks and whites
  separated

½ cup vegetable oil

2 tablespoons vanilla extract

¼ teaspoon cream of tartar

## ASSEMBLY AND
## ICING

Powdered sugar, to taste

5 ounces mini
  marshmallows

14 ounces chocolate
  frosting, whipped

help keep the parchment in place and keep the cake from sticking to the parchment as well as the sides of the pan.

**3.** Whisk the cake flour, sugar, baking powder, and salt together in large, wide bowl.

**4.** Combine the hot chocolate mix and water, mixing well.

**5.** Stir together the egg yolks, oil, vanilla, and hot chocolate mixture, then add the wet mixture to the flour mixture and whisk until well combined.

**6.** Using a stand mixer fitted with a whisk attachment, or for the truly tenacious, a handheld whisk, whip the egg whites and cream of tartar until foamy. Increase the mixer's speed and whip until stiff peaks form.

**7.** Fold the whipped egg whites into the batter in thirds until no white remains. A silicone or rubber spatula works great for this.

**8.** Pour the batter onto the prepared baking sheet and spread it evenly across the pan.

**9.** Lift the baking sheet a couple inches over a table or counter and let it drop a couple times to release any large air bubbles.

**10.** Bake until the cake springs back when pressed lightly in the center, 12 to 15 minutes.

**11.** When the cake is done baking, run a knife around the edges to ensure it won't stick to the pan.

## ASSEMBLY AND ICING

**1.** While the cake is still warm (and ideally as soon as you're able to lift it safely), cut a piece of parchment paper slightly larger than your pan.

**2.** Sprinkle the top of the cake generously with powdered sugar.

**3.** Place the parchment over the sugar, then cover with a wire rack and invert the cake onto the wire rack.

**4.** Starting from the long side, gently roll the warm cake, parchment and all, into a spiral.

**5.** Let the rolled cake cool, seam side down, for 1 hour.

**6.** Carefully unroll the cake, removing the top parchment, and spread the filling across the cake, followed by a generous sprinkle of marshmallows across the filling.

**7.** Roll the cake back up and lift it off the bottom parchment.

**8.** Spread chocolate frosting over the cake, then sprinkle it lightly with powdered sugar, like a dusting of snow!

# Strawberry Jelly Roll Cake SERVES 8

Strawberries are the food of magical folk, and there are wonderful traditions of folklore to remind us of this. In Bavaria farmers tie baskets of strawberries to the horns of their cows as an offering to elves in hopes of healthy calves and increased milk production. Bean-Tighe are magical folk in Ireland who will watch over your house for you and even help with chores if you leave out their favorite food for them to find. That favorite food is, of course, strawberries! In fact, no matter where you are, if you enter a room and smell strawberries but cannot find any, you can be guaranteed fairies have recently been visiting.

With all that in mind, this cake was made for two of the most magical small people in my life: Kiran and Sivan, the twin daughters of some dear friends. The girls had asked me to make them a "pink cake," and I couldn't imagine a better assignment. I made them a cake filled with what I wish for them: a vanilla sponge to bring self-empowerment, and strawberries so they can feel my never-ending love. (Also, the continued dedication to always be willing to make them any color cake they could possibly wish for.)

## FILLING

24 ounces strawberries

Juice of 1 lemon

1 tablespoon gelatin
  powder

1 cup powdered sugar

4 cups heavy cream

2 tablespoons vanilla extract

*Ingredients continued on
  page 254*

## FILLING

**1.** Chop two-thirds of the strawberries into quarters and place the pieces in a small food processor or blender. Process or blend to create a purée. If desired, run the purée through a fine sieve to remove the seeds.

**2.** Place the lemon juice in a small pot set over high heat and bring to a boil.

**3.** Add the gelatin and whisk vigorously until the gelatin is completely dissolved.

**4.** Remove the lemon juice and gelatin mixture from the heat and mix in the strawberry purée.

**5.** Transfer the mixture to a covered container and place in the refrigerator for a couple hours, or until

## CAKE

1 ⅓ cups cake flour

¾ cup sugar

1 ½ teaspoons baking
   powder

¼ teaspoon salt

5 eggs, yolks and white
   separated

½ cup vegetable oil, and
   more for greasing the pan

4 tablespoons vanilla extract

¼ cup

¼ teaspoons cream of tartar

## ASSEMBLY

Powdered sugar, to taste

thickened. You can also make this a day ahead of time and simply let it thicken overnight.

**6.** In a large bowl, combine the strawberry purée with the powdered sugar, heavy cream, and vanilla.

**7.** Using an electric mixer, beat on high until smooth with medium peaks.

**8.** Place the mixture in the refrigerator and allow to set for at least 2 hours. You can also make this up to a day ahead.

## CAKE

**1.** Adjust your oven's rack to a middle position and preheat the oven to 350°F.

**2.** Lightly grease a 13-by-18-inch rimmed baking sheet, line it with parchment paper, and lightly grease the parchment. It feels repetitive but will help keep the parchment in place and keep the cake from sticking to the parchment as well as the sides of the pan.

**3.** Whisk the cake flour, sugar, baking powder, and salt together in large, wide bowl.

**4.** In a medium bowl, stir together the egg yolks, oil, vanilla, and water, then add the wet mixture to the flour mixture. Stir until well combined.

**5.** Using a stand mixer fitted with a whisk attachment—or, for the truly tenacious, a handheld whisk—whip the egg whites and cream of tartar on medium speed until foamy. Once foamy, increase the mixer's speed and whip until stiff peaks form.

**6.** Fold the whipped egg whites into the batter in

thirds until no white remains. A silicone or rubber spatula works great for this.

**7.** Pour the batter onto the prepared baking sheet and spread evenly across the pan.

**8.** Lift the baking sheet a couple inches over a table or counter and let drop a couple times to release any large air bubbles.

**9.** Bake until the cake springs back when pressed lightly in the center, 12 to 15 minutes.

**10.** While the cake is baking, finely chop the remaining strawberries and then set them aside.

**11.** When the cake is done baking, run a knife around the edges to ensure it won't stick to the pan.

### ASSEMBLY

**1.** While the cake is still warm, cut a piece of parchment paper slightly larger than your cake pan.

**2.** Sprinkle the top of the cake generously with powdered sugar, then place the parchment over the sugar. Cover with a wire rack.

**3.** Invert the cake onto the wire rack and then starting from the long side, gently roll the warm cake. (There will be parchment on both sides of the cake.)

**4.** Let the rolled cake cool, seam side down, for 1 hour.

**5.** Carefully unroll the cake, remove the top parchment, and spread the strawberry cream filling across the cake. Sprinkle the chopped strawberries on top of the filling.

**6.** Roll the cake back up, gently lifting it from the bottom parchment, then sprinkle more powdered sugar generously over the cake.

# Pumpkin Jelly Roll Cake with Maple Cream SERVES 8

An amalgamation of balance and generosity, prosperity and protection, the maple and pumpkin in this recipe roll together to create a warm and wonderful gift. Topped with candied pecans for a little sweet success, it is a gift that will keep giving.

## CANDIED PECANS

2 tablespoons salted butter

3 cups pecan halves

½ packed cup light brown sugar

1 ¼ teaspoons kosher salt or sea salt

½ teaspoon cinnamon powder

¼ cup water

1 teaspoon vanilla extract

## FILLING

2 cups heavy cream

8 ounces cream cheese, softened

¼ cup maple sugar

¼ cup powdered sugar

*Ingredients continued on page 259*

## CANDIED PECANS

**1.** Preheat your oven to 350°F. Line a baking sheet with parchment paper and set aside.

**2.** Melt the butter in a large skillet set over medium heat. Add the pecans and stir continuously for 3 minutes to lightly toast.

**3.** Once toasted, add the brown sugar and stir until melted.

**4.** Stir in the salt and cinnamon until well distributed, then add the water. Stir continuously until the water evaporates.

**5.** Add the vanilla and stir until evenly coated.

**6.** Spread the mixture evenly across the prepared baking sheet and bake for 5 to 7 minutes, until fragrant and just crisp.

**7.** Remove the pecans from the oven and allow to cool completely.

## CAKE

Baking spray

1 ⅓ cups cake flour

¾ packed cup dark brown
  sugar

1 ½ teaspoons baking
  powder

¼ teaspoon salt

5 eggs, yolks and whites
  separated

½ cup vegetable oil

¼ cup canned pumpkin
  puree

2 tablespoons vanilla extract

½ teaspoon pumpkin pie
  spice

¼ teaspoon cream of tartar

## ASSEMBLY

Powdered sugar, to taste

14 ounces store-bought
  cream cheese frosting (1
  standard-size tub)

## FILLING

**1.** Place all the filling ingredients in a large bowl and beat on high with a hand or stand mixer until smooth with medium peaks.

**2.** Place the filling in the refrigerator and allow to set for at least 2 hours. You can also make and refrigerate it up to a day ahead of time.

## CAKE

**1.** Adjust your oven's rack to a middle position and preheat the oven to 350°F.

**2.** Lightly spray a 13-by-18-inch rimmed baking sheet with baking spray, line it with parchment paper, and then lightly spray the parchment. It feels repetitive but will help keep the parchment in place and keep the cake from sticking to the parchment as well as the sides of the pan.

**3.** Whisk the cake flour, brown sugar, baking powder, and salt together in a large, wide bowl.

**4.** Whisk the egg yolks, oil, pumpkin, vanilla, and pumpkin pie spice into the flour mixture until well combined.

**5.** Using a stand mixer fitted with a whisk attachment or, for the truly tenacious, a handheld whisk, whip the egg whites and cream of tartar on medium speed until foamy. Increase the speed to high and whip until stiff peaks form.

**6.** Fold the whipped egg whites into the batter in thirds until no white remains. A silicone or rubber spatula works great for this.

**7.** Pour the batter onto the prepared baking sheet and spread it evenly across the pan.

**8.** Lift the baking sheet a couple inches over a table or counter and let it drop a couple times to release any large air bubbles.

**9.** Bake until the cake springs back when pressed lightly in its center, 12 to 15 minutes.

**10.** When the cake is done baking, run a knife around the edges to ensure it won't stick to the pan.

### ASSEMBLY

**1.** While the cake is still warm, cut a piece of parchment paper slightly larger than your pan.

**2.** Sprinkle the top of the cake generously with powdered sugar.

**3.** Place the parchment over the sugar, then cover with a wire rack and invert the cake onto the wire rack.

**4.** Starting from the long side, gently roll the warm cake. (There will be parchment on both sides of the cake.)

**5.** Let the rolled cake cool, seam side down, for 1 hour. Once cool, carefully unroll, removing the top piece of parchment paper, and spread the cream filling across the cake.

**6.** Roll the cake back up, then spread the cream cheese frosting over the cake and cover with candied pecans.

The candied pecans can be prepared ahead of time, and honestly, you could use any kind of nut you favor. We particularly like pecans, though, and I always make extra as a snack for my husband.

LIGHT, FIRE, AND ABUNDANCE

# Citrus-Cello MAKES APPROXIMATELY 6 SMALL GLASSES

One year for Wylie's eighth birthday, we spent four days hiking the Cinque Terre in Italy. It was beautiful and wondrous and everything we had hoped it would be. It was also a lot of hiking. So. Much. Hiking. Sam was in his element, though, and the kids and I were bribed with the exact right amount of copious gelato to find our element too.

On one of the hiking days, Sam connected with an old man sitting beneath a tent in his vineyard. The man leaned on a small rickety folding table that looked like it was close to collapsing from the weight of recycled jam jars filled with a sunny, bright liquid. Over the course of an extended conversation wherein neither party spoke the other's language, Sam became the owner of one of those jam jars of limoncello. He still speaks today of how delicious (and potent) that trailside hooch was, and I, admittedly, know my cocktails will never reach such grandeur. However, whenever I make these bottles of citrusy liqueur, I am immediately back in those days of salty air and lush, winding pathways, of sticky, gelato-covered smiles and gorgeous sunsets. Of days that feel never-ending, and joyously so.

As sometimes our "something sweet" is less a fork and plate and more a chilled glass and ice, I offer this up to you for the evenings the kids go to bed early, the late afternoons of friends gathering, and the brunches that welcome a sunny day.

8 blood oranges, or 6 grapefruits, or 3 lemons and 4 limes, or 10 lemons

24 ounces vodka

2 cups sugar

2 cups water

**1.** Peel the skins off of the citrus fruit of your choice, removing as much of the pith from the skins as possible. (The pith is the white lining between the peel and the fruit and can add some bitterness to the flavor.)

**2.** Place the peels in the bottom of a large jar.

**3.** Pour the vodka over the peels, making sure all the peel pieces are completely covered by the vodka.

**4.** Tightly seal the jar and store it in a cool, dry place for at least 1 week. I often store mine for about 10 days—storing longer won't hurt and can add some flavor, but I have found anything over 14 weeks doesn't give you much flavor return on time investment.

**5.** Combine the sugar and water in a small saucepan set over high heat and bring to a boil.

**6.** Lower the heat and let simmer for 3 minutes, until the sugar is completely dissolved. This is your simple syrup.

**7.** Refrigerate the simple syrup until you are ready to combine it with the infused vodka.

**8.** Once the peels are done steeping in the vodka, pour the liquid through a cheesecloth or fine strainer to remove any residual solids.

**9.** Combine the vodka with 1 cup simple syrup. Taste and adjust the syrup or vodka level as needed.

**10.** Drink immediately or store for up to a few days. I find that it tastes best if I let the final combination of vodka and syrup sit for a couple days to mellow out a bit.

LIGHT, FIRE, AND ABUNDANCE

*Awesome Sauce*

# SAUCES AND CONDIMENTS

**SURE, WE COULD LIVE** in a world without that little bit of something extra, without the little cup on the side, but why would we want to? Sauces and condiments add exactly what we need to bring a meal together. They are a small something that unites. Easily forgotten, at times shoved to the side, but perfect to give a little push into new territory. Here it's not just about what's expected, what the main line might be in the narrative; it's adding a touch that turns into a game changer. A touch that may be tiny in stature but can be big with intent. Share some courage, bestow a little protection, open a heart just a bit. Kindly pour some love into a rough wound. Put forth the smallest reminder that there is greatness. In you. In them. In this amazing moment. It is ripe for recognition if we don't go too fast or ignore too much, if we're willing to put in the smallest of extra efforts.

# Hot Honey MAKES ABOUT 1 CUP OR 8 OUNCES

Honey itself seems pretty magical all on its own, when I take the time to really think about it. Cultivated by bees and made from the nectar of their particular location, it can have endless variations, each particular to the hive and each with its own unique taste, its own specific profile.

Not only that, but honey can also be used in innumerable ways, including to smooth, sweeten, and salve. And with no expiration date, honey on your shelf can provide comfort and delight for as long as you have it on hand.

There's something I love about combining the calming sweetness of honey with the fiery energy of peppers. There is of course the deliciously inevitable sweet and spicy flavor outcome, but even more wonderfully, there's the spiritual powerhouse of two ingredients that both ignite passion and protection. Honey, in all its tranquil relief, combined with the courageous intensity of peppers, creates a mixture that is truly spellbinding.

## TRADITIONAL

3 fresh habanero peppers

6 whole dried red chili peppers

1 cup honey (see Tip)

¼ teaspoon red wine vinegar

When measuring the honey, use baking spray in the measuring cup to keep the honey from sticking.

**1.** Roughly chop your peppers, removing the stems but leaving the seeds. *When I say roughly, I mean it—don't worry about whether the sections are uniform or the cuts are clean. We just want to open the peppers up for better absorption. The dried chili peppers are small enough that you can often just cut them in half or split them down the middle. With the habaneros I sometimes simply cut them in quarters with my shears. Remember to thoroughly wash your hands and all items the peppers touch before moving on with the recipe. The juice, even from mild peppers, can be discomforting in the wrong place. If the worst does happen, rinse with milk.*

**2.** Combine the honey and peppers in a small saucepan. Stir well so they are well combined and the peppers are not on the surface.

**3.** Turn the heat to medium and bring to a healthy bubble.

**4.** Reduce the heat and keep a low but steady simmer for 4 to 7 minutes. You want the peppers to have a chance to steep while keeping the temperature fairly low to avoid burning.

**5.** Turn off the heat, add the vinegar, and stir well.

**6.** Let cool for at least 5 minutes.

**7.** Cover the top of your container with cheesecloth (I hold mine on with a rubber band) and pour the honey through to strain it into a clean container with a lid.

**8.** Let sit, uncovered, until completely cool, then attach the lid. This will keep in a cool, dry place for up to 6 months.

## SHISHITO

SHARP AND A BIT GRASSY, THE PEPPER FLAVOR IS FANTASTIC IN THIS AND PRODUCES VERY LITTLE HEAT.

HEAT 0, FLAVOR 5

7 fresh shishito peppers, roughly chopped

1 cup honey

¼ teaspoon red wine vinegar

Perfect for dumplings, wontons, and noodles

## SERRANO

A FRESH, BRIGHT, AND EARTHY PEPPER FLAVOR THAT IS LIGHT IN HEAT.

HEAT 1, FLAVOR 5

5 fresh serrano peppers, roughly chopped

1 cup honey

¼ teaspoon red wine vinegar

Perfect for Italian salads and garlic bread

---

*Tip*

While this recipe will result in an amazing traditional hot honey, I encourage you to experiment with your favorite peppers to create your own perfect sweetly peppered concoction. Simply follow the directions while substituting the peppers of your choice. For guidance, dried peppers make for thicker honey; fresh peppers result in slightly thinner, more saucy honey. See below for my recommendations for variants. Flavors and heat are rated on a scale of 1 (low) to 5 (high).

## HOLLAND

FRUITY AND SWEET WITH MILD HEAT.

HEAT 1, FLAVOR 4

4 fresh Holland peppers, roughly chopped

1 cup honey

¼ teaspoon red wine vinegar

Perfect for Sweet Potato Fries (see page 159), focaccia, and savory
  breakfast bakes

## ANCHO AND POBLANO

SMOKY, BUT WITH MILD HEAT.

HEAT 2, FLAVOR 2

4 dried ancho chili peppers, roughly chopped

1 fresh poblano pepper, roughly chopped

1 cup honey

¼ teaspoon red wine vinegar

Perfect for Crispy Chicken (see page 65), pulled pork sandwiches, and
  Black Pepper Biscuits (see page 58)

## HABANERO

HOT IN HEAT AND HIGH IN FLAVOR, THIS CITRUSY COMBO IS NOT FOR
THE FAINT OF HEART.

HEAT 4.5, FLAVOR 4.5

6 fresh Habanero peppers, roughly chopped

1 cup honey

¼ teaspoon red wine vinegar

Perfect for Crispy Chicken (see page 65) and Sausage Pesto Rolls (see
  page 185)

# Simple Marinara

This marinara is easy to make, but don't think the simplicity makes it any less divine. In fact, making it offers the perfect moment to appreciate that sometimes the simplest acts, or recipes, can add up to great things. In the case of this marinara, the tomatoes and onion in the sauce reveal possibilities for love and friendship, the oregano and basil promise joy and love, while the parsley and garlic ease whatever grief may have come before and protect against its return. Consider it a sauce (and a moment) to let go of the disappointments of the past and look forward with hope to the opportunities that lie ahead.

½ cup diced white onion

4 garlic cloves, minced

2 tablespoons olive oil

28 ounces canned crushed
   tomatoes

2 tablespoons garlic
   powder

1 teaspoon dried basil

1 teaspoon dried oregano

1 teaspoon dried parsley

¼ teaspoon salt, or more
   to taste

**1.** In a medium saucepan set over medium heat, sauté the onion and garlic in olive oil until fragrant, about 3 minutes.

**2.** Add the tomatoes, garlic powder, basil, oregano, parsley, and salt and bring to a simmer.

**3.** Continue to simmer for 20 minutes.

**4.** Pour into an airtight container and let come to room temperature.

**5.** Store in the refrigerator and use within 1 week.

# Spicy Arrabbiata Sauce MAKES ABOUT 1 1/4 CUPS OR 10 OUNCES

This spicy sauce is all about the flow of energy, the passion to pursue, and the infinite possibilities that live inside us. It challenges us to live up to our potential, to push against the expected, to not simply settle for what comes easily. We must have the courage to be all that we are capable of, to give the world what we alone can give, and to remember that we have the dust of stars in our bones. As you stir this over the heat of your stove, stoke the fire in your heart.

½ cup chopped red onion

6 garlic cloves, minced

2 tablespoons olive oil

14 ½ ounces canned petite diced tomatoes

¾ cup vegetable broth

1 tablespoon tamari or traditional soy sauce

2 tablespoons nutritional yeast

1 teaspoon red pepper flakes, or more to taste

1 teaspoon garlic powder

1 teaspoon onion powder

1 teaspoon dried oregano

½ teaspoon salt

½ teaspoon black pepper

¼ teaspoon baking powder

**1.** In a medium saucepan set over medium heat, sauté the onion and garlic in olive oil until fragrant, about 3 minutes.

**2.** Add the rest of the ingredients and bring to a simmer.

**3.** Continue to simmer for 7 minutes.

**4.** Pour into an airtight container and let come to room temperature.

**5.** Store in the refrigerator and use within 1 week.

tomato

opens the heart

# Bolognese Sauce MAKES ABOUT 2 CUPS OR 16 OUNCES

While this sauce is perfect any time of year, I always make big batches of it for the fall harvest festivals. That time of year always feels meant for collection and curation of what's important. It is a time to be grateful for the things we're getting right and the love, hope, and support we have in our lives, and hold all of that close. The fall season is a chance to revel in what we have sown and nurtured to fruition throughout the spring and summer: our family, our art, and our work. It is a time to gather in that which gives us strength and inspiration and preserve it to put to use through the darker months.

Inspired to revel in what we have grown in our tiny garden, every year at this time, our family makes giant pots of spaghetti sauce to have throughout the winter. We use almost every vegetable we have grown in our little plot of soil in the middle of New York City, recognizing how our hard work has in turn given us this bounty. We have our last feast from our little garden plot and save the rest for a bit of brightness in the cold. The kids help gather the tomatoes and herbs. We cut the last blooms of our roses. We set a table ripe with our hard work and love.

While the ingredients for this sauce are common enough to have come from any garden, they combine for a special cast of openheartedness and infinite possibility, joy and prosperity, and creativity and tenacity. This is a combination that is exceptionally celebratory for the end of a summer and a brilliant way to head forth on a new path toward the end of the year. It's a wonderful sauce for the in-between spaces of our lives, a chance to stand firmly in the present, with gratitude for all that came before and all that awaits us.

1 pint cherry tomatoes, halved

Ingredients continued on page 274

**1.** Preheat your oven to 350°F.

**2.** On a large baking pan, toss the cherry tomatoes in 2 tablespoons olive oil and generous amounts of salt and pepper. Bake until roasted, 25 to 30 minutes, or

OPPOSITE, TOP TO BOTTOM: SPICY ARRABBIATA SAUCE (SEE PAGE 271), BOLOGNESE SAUCE, AND SIMPLE MARINARA (SEE PAGE 270).

¼ cup olive oil, divided, and
more for browning the
meat

Salt, to taste

Black pepper, to taste

1 Spanish onion, diced

5 to 8 garlic cloves, minced

28 ounces tomatoes,
canned and crushed
or fresh and roughly
chopped

4 carrots, diced

2 zucchini, sliced

1 red bell pepper, chopped

1 yellow bell pepper,
chopped

2 tablespoons chopped
fresh oregano

2 tablespoons chopped
fresh basil

2 tablespoons chopped
fresh parsley

1 pound ground bison or
sirloin

1 pound sweet-and-hot
sausage, casings removed

5 ounces garlic-and-herb
cream cheese

until they are just this side of having burned edges.
Set aside.

**3.** Cover the bottom of a large saucepan with the
remaining 2 tablespoons olive oil and heat to just
steaming, 1 to 2 minutes.

**4.** Add the onion and garlic and cook, stirring
occasionally, over medium heat until soft and
fragrant, 3 to 5 minutes.

**5.** Pour in the crushed or chopped tomatoes and stir
for a few minutes, then let simmer for 45 minutes
to 1 hour.

**6.** Add the carrots, zucchini, and bell peppers.

**7.** Continue to simmer as you add half the fresh
herbs. The mixture will be thick, but we'll blend it all
together in a bit.

**8.** Finally, add the roasted cherry tomatoes
and cover.

**9.** Simmer for 45 minutes. *I like to take the lid off
for the last 20 minutes or so to fill our apartment with
delicious smells and revel in the aroma of the sauce. Doing
so will also help thicken the sauce a bit. I love both effects of
removing the lid. But that's just me. You do you.*

**10.** Smooth the sauce to your desired consistency
either by using an immersion blender or by letting
the sauce cool, pouring it in batches into a blender,
and pulse-blending each batch a few times. (Due to
a tragic mishap while taking apart an immersion
blender on Halloween 2011, I rarely use ours and
at this point I go with option two; either, however, is fine.)

**11.** Before serving, brown the ground bison (or sirloin) and sausages in a separate pan with a small amount of olive oil to keep them from sticking. Drain the grease well.

**12.** Add the meat to the sauce, along with the cream cheese, and stir until the cream cheese melts.

**13.** Add the rest of the fresh herbs and serve.

*Tip*

You can use whatever herbs sound delicious to you—the oregano, basil, and parsley are just what we've managed to successfully grow in our small garden. Regardless of what herbs you use, bunch them together and then twist them, as it makes them easier to chop.

# Pesto

Pesto was the first recipe I ever intentionally made my own. I played around with various combinations of ingredients, and I clearly remember the very first time Samaire and Wylie told me they preferred my pesto over store-bought ones. It filled my heart to bursting. Knowing I had somehow put together something so simply—something they called "Mama's pesto"—was enough for me to begin trying to make, and remake, all kinds of dishes. Dishes they would know I had made just for them. Where the ingredients and amounts were selected to make them smile.

There's not a lot of complexity to pesto, but it will always be one of my favorite things to make. All because of the small voices that one night asked, "Do we get to have Mama's pesto?" with excitement and joy.

## SPINACH WALNUT PESTO

MAKES ABOUT 1 CUP OR 8 OUNCES

Walnuts are all about exoneration. Make this pesto when you're ready to let go of an old habit, release some worries, or break a stream of downward luck. It's the perfect complement to a night under a waning moon.

5 ounces spinach

¼ cup grated pecorino cheese

4 garlic gloves

1 ¾ cups walnuts

⅔ cup olive oil

½ teaspoon salt, or to taste

**1.** Combine all the ingredients in a food processor or blender (I find layering them in the order listed works best), and blend until your desired consistency is reached.

**2.** Store in the refrigerator for up to 1 week or freeze in premeasured quantities for up to 6 months.

## BASIL PINE NUT PESTO

MAKES ABOUT 1 CUP OR 8 OUNCES

Bright and light, this pesto filled with pine nuts brings spiritual consciousness and enlightenment. Spin some of this up for moments when you are searching for a bit of inspiration or peace in your heart. Make yourself the kind of meal that has you feeling the echo of the stars in your bones.

3 ounces fresh basil

⅓ cup Parmesan cheese

2 garlic cloves

¼ cup pine nuts

½ cup olive oil

Salt, to taste

**1.** Combine all the ingredients in a food processor or blender (I find layering them in the order listed works best), and blend until your desired consistency is reached.

**2.** Store in the refrigerator for up to 1 week or freeze in premeasured quantities for up to 6 months.

## KALE PUMPKIN SEED PESTO

MAKES ABOUT 1 CUP OR 8 OUNCES

This pesto summons the earthiness of autumn, promising prosperity and protection against any bitterness that may occur, in the meal or in the environment. It's thick and rich, and a fantastic topping on homemade bread or dolloped atop a hearty plate of gnocchi.

1 ½ ounces kale

1 ½ ounces Asiago cheese

2 garlic cloves

½ cup pepitas (shell-free
  pumpkin seeds)

½ cup olive oil

Salt, to taste

**1.** Combine all the ingredients in a food processor or blender (I find layering them in the order listed works best), and blend until your desired consistency is reached.

**2.** Store in the refrigerator for up to 1 week or freeze in premeasured quantities for up to 6 months.

# Salsa Verde Makes about 1 cup or 8 ounces

If only we could always be sure of our hearts—what we wish to do, how we wish to do it, or who we want to be to those around us. It is not always easy to have courage in ourselves. It's so much easier to believe in those we love and their endless possibilities. It is a much more difficult thing not just to see but to truly believe in our own potential.

The tomatillos here steady the heart, the peppers lend courage, and the onion recalls our layered presence in this world and the promise in our multifaceted being. We are no one thing; we are more than the roles and expectations laid before us. We have the passion and energy to be courageous in our existence. Draw upon all that defines you as you assemble this concoction of ingredients to remind you, wholly, of how amazing you are.

8 tomatillos

1 white onion, quartered

2 garlic cloves, minced

1 serrano pepper, diced

2 tablespoons finely
chopped fresh cilantro

¼ teaspoon salt, or more
to taste

**1.** Preheat the oven to 400°F.

**2.** Peel off the papery husks from the tomatillos, then rinse the tomatillos to remove any sticky residue. Cut each tomatillo in half.

**3.** Place the tomatillos on a baking sheet and roast in the oven for 10 minutes, turning them over once. The skins should develop a golden brown color.

**4.** Combine the tomatillos and all remaining ingredients in a blender or food processor and blend until your desired consistency is reached. We like it a bit chunky, so I use the machine only briefly to break everything up a bit. If you want it smoother, let the processor or blender run for a minute.

**5.** Add salt to taste, if needed.

# Pecorino Pepper Sauce MAKES ABOUT 3/4 CUP OR 6 OUNCES

This sauce is spicy and indulgent, smooth and distinctive. Its combination of the coolness of cream with the spicy energy of cracked black pepper will leave you ready to banish negativity and create space for true happiness.

3 tablespoons unsalted butter

1 ½ tablespoons all-purpose flour

¾ cup chicken broth or vegetable broth

1 cup heavy cream

1 ½ teaspoons black pepper

½ teaspoon dried oregano

½ teaspoon dried basil

1 ¾ cups shredded pecorino cheese

Salt, to taste (optional)

**1.** In a pot set over medium heat, melt the butter while whisking in the flour. This will make your roux and keep your sauce thick. *Reflect on how sometimes the smallest steps up front pay big dividends. Steps like making a roux or even just making time for yourself. It feels almost inconsequential in the moment, but it often doesn't take long to reap the benefits. So as you stir the butter and flour, watching them gather and combine, think about how you might take time to gather yourself. Give to yourself in a small way, so you can give to the world in a bigger way down the road.*

**2.** Once the flour is fully combined with the butter (no white showing), slowly pour in the broth 1/4 cup at a time, while continuing to whisk to keep the texture smooth.

**3.** Lower the heat, pour in the cream, and whisk to combine.

**4.** Add the pepper, oregano, and basil while continuing to whisk.

**5.** Add the pecorino and stir to incorporate it as it melts.

**6.** Because the pecorino is salty, you will want to taste the sauce now and see how you'd like to season it. I don't usually add salt, but a pinch now can help enliven the flavors if you feel something is missing!

# Chipotle Mayo MAKES ABOUT 1 CUP OR 8 OUNCES

Absolutely perfect for a meal of Black Bean Burgers (see page 133) and Sweet Potato Fries (see page 159), this smoky mayo is as easy to make as it is tasty. With peppers adding a boost of courage and a dash of lime for luck, this small act of intention serves all kinds of moments.

4 canned chipotle chili
  peppers in adobo sauce,
  drained and chopped

½ cup mayonnaise

½ cup sour cream

2 tablespoons lime juice

**1.** Using an immersion blender or a small food processor, combine all ingredients until the mayonnaise is smooth.

**2.** Place the resulting mayo into an airtight container and store in the refrigerator for up to 2 weeks.

# BBQ Sauce MAKES ABOUT 1 CUP OR 8 OUNCES

BBQ sauce is a fantastically varied condiment. You can often tell where someone grew up by their preference in flavor: whether it's spicy, smoky, sweet, or tangy, everyone has their "perfect sauce." This one is ours. It serves us all year round, on the sunny summer vacations where we're lucky enough to rent a house with a grill, or on star-filled chilly evenings spent making the perfect deep-dish pizza in our tiny apartment.

A tiny bit sweet, a little spicy, this sauce reflects who we are as a family—many a test pot was concocted until we got just the right combination of flavors everyone loved. I encourage you to play with this recipe, adding honey or more peppers, a little liquid smoke or a touch more vinegar, to create your own just-right sauce.

2 tablespoons olive oil

1 Vidalia onion, chopped

2 jalapeños, chopped

Salt, to taste

Black pepper, to taste

3 garlic cloves, minced

1 teaspoon smoked paprika

1 teaspoon dried thyme

1 teaspoon dried oregano

1 cup ketchup

¼ cup yellow mustard

2 tablespoons
  Worcestershire sauce

1 tablespoon white vinegar

⅔ packed cup brown sugar

**1.** In a pot set over medium heat, combine the olive oil, onion, jalapeños, and a sprinkle of salt and pepper to taste.

**2.** Sauté until the onion pieces are translucent and tender, 5 to 7 minutes, while stirring regularly.

**3.** Add the garlic, paprika, thyme, and oregano and toast for about 1 minute.

**4.** Add the ketchup, mustard, Worcestershire sauce, vinegar, and brown sugar.

**5.** Raise the heat to medium-high and simmer, stirring frequently, for 5 minutes.

**6.** If you want the sauce to be smoother, transfer it to a blender or small food processor and pulse until it reaches your desired consistency.

**7.** Store in a jar with a tight-fitting lid in the refrigerator for up to 2 weeks.

# Honey Mustard MAKES ABOUT 3/4 CUP OR 6 OUNCES

While it's easy to grab a honey mustard off the shelf at the store, I really enjoy making my own. This version can be used as a dip or dressing and tastes wonderful alongside Crispy Chicken (see page 65), but it's also delicious with Savory Waffles (see page 30). Regardless of how a jar of this might find its way to your table, the intentions it carries are universal. It is a sweet reminder that small acts can become great and that the little things we do for each other can matter more than we may ever know. So pass the honey mustard and pay forward as much good as you can.

⅓ cup Dijon mustard

¼ cup honey

¼ cup mayonnaise

1 tablespoon lemon juice

¼ teaspoon cayenne
  powder

**1.** Combine all the ingredients in a blender or food processor and blend until fully combined. You can also just use a bowl and fork, which works just as well—you just want to make sure everything is combined well so that you can no longer see traces of any single ingredient.

**2.** Store refrigerated in an airtight container for up to 6 months.

# Gingered Ketchup MAKES ABOUT 1 1/2 CUPS OR 12 OUNCES

Ketchup, usually a fairly nondescript and ordinary condiment, finds new life in this version with added spices and seasonings. The ginger and shallots are sure to draw adventure and cure any misfortune along the way.

1 cup ketchup

2 tablespoons liquid aminos
  or soy sauce

1 tablespoon
  Worcestershire sauce

¼ cup roughly chopped
  shallot

2 tablespoons minced fresh
  ginger

1 packed tablespoon brown
  sugar

½ teaspoon garlic powder

**1.** Combine all the ingredients in a blender or food processor and blend until fully combined.

**2.** Store refrigerated in an airtight container for up to 3 weeks.

# Cilantro Purée MAKES ABOUT 3/4 CUP OR 6 OUNCES

With jalapeños providing protection and cilantro inciting passion, add this sauce to any meal you make for someone you love before they head out on a new adventure. Adjust the quantity of jalapeños according to your own heat tolerance.

2 bunches cilantro
(approximately 2 packed cups)

7 to 9 pickled jalapeños, to taste

¼ cup and 2 tablespoons brine from jalapeños

**1.** Place all the ingredients in a food processor or blender and blend until well combined.

**2.** Store in an airtight container in the refrigerator and use within a few days.

# Simple Salad Dressing MAKES ABOUT 1/3 CUP OR 2 1/2 OUNCES

Salad dressing is one of those items that are simple enough to buy, but once you make your own it's *really* hard to go back to store-bought. Easy to make and store, it's a nice addition to your homemade rotation. This particular version is filled with ingredients that lend courage and protection, big intentions for what can be a quick, simple dish. It's perfect atop an arugula salad and placed next to eggs to start the day or during a waxing moon as we build toward a life we love and the person we most want to be.

3 tablespoons olive oil

1 tablespoon apple cider
  vinegar or red wine
  vinegar

1 teaspoon Dijon mustard

1 teaspoon honey

2 small garlic cloves,
  pressed or minced, or 1
  teaspoon garlic powder

½ teaspoon fine sea salt

¼ teaspoon black pepper

¼ teaspoon red pepper
  flakes

**1.** Combine all the ingredients in a jar with a lid and tightly seal.

**2.** Put on your favorite joyful song, turn it just a touch too loud, and shake the jar vigorously until its ingredients are completely combined. *If you have had "a day," it might take more than one song. Regardless, sing as loud as you want, dance as ridiculously as you can, and if someone walks in, let them know you're making dinner. Because even the most mundane of tasks can give us a moment of joyful reprieve from time to time. And God knows we deserve it. You deserve it. So shake that booty, friend. And the jar. Make sure you also shake the jar.*

**3.** Serve immediately or store in the refrigerator for up to 1 week. If you refrigerate the dressing, give it a good solid shake before serving.

# Before You Go

**I'VE NEVER BEEN ONE** to believe there was only one way to do things, only one correct approach. It's what led me all those decades ago to being a witch. I needed a spiritual path with guides but not rules. I needed to find my own way, build my own practice, so I could best feed and share my own heart and soul. I believe we all have something unique to give, unique stories to share, rare light the world needs. This book, I hope, will help you find your own magic, even if it's simply in the kitchen, over bowls and crumbs and the everyday of life. It is not meant to be a directive but an instigation, a place to begin exploring and learning so you too can indulge and share what speaks to your heart and feeds your soul.

Timers run down, dishes are passed, plates are cleared, meals end . . . the magic endures.

# Acknowledgments

**ALL MY GRATITUDE GOES** to my New York family. You have shared endless meals and wonder-filled nights with us and shown up time and again to laugh, tell stories, and try one more bite. There will always be seats at our table for all of you.

A world of thanks, as well, to Jenny Memmott, cousin-in-law extraordinaire, amazing friend, and best possible sous chef. I never would have survived that week without you. Though I'm sure my side still hurts from all that laughter.

And last, but certainly not least, thanks to Sam, my whole heart. You started all this with an anniversary gift, but the gift you give me every day is what makes it possible. Your belief in me holds me up and gives me space to dream bigger than I have ever thought possible. You are where all my magic originates. I can't wait to spend endless lifetimes making memory-filled meals with you.

# Recipe Index